Golf, Grandkids, and Giant Sunglasses

Your Guide to Financial Security
and Peace of Mind in Retirement

Derek Colton

Golf, Grandkids, and Giant Sunglasses
Your Guide to Financial Security and Peace of Mind in Retirement

© 2020 Derek Colton
All rights reserved.
ISBN: 978-1-946203-77-9
Cover designed by Freepik.

Disclaimer

The information provided in this book is for informational purposes only and is not intended to be a source of advice or credit analysis with respect to the material presented. The information and/or documents contained in this book do not constitute legal or financial advice and should never be used without first consulting with an insurance and/or a financial professional to determine what may be best for your individual needs.

The publisher and the author do not make any guarantee or other promise as to any results that may be obtained from using the content of this book. You should never make any investment decision without first consulting with your own financial advisor and conducting your own research and due diligence. To the maximum extent permitted by law, the publisher and the author disclaim any and all liability in the event any information, commentary, analysis, opinions, advice, and/or recommendations contained in this book prove to be inaccurate, incomplete or unreliable, or result in any investment or other losses.

Although the author and publisher have made every effort to ensure that the information in this book was correct at press time, the author and publisher do not assume and hereby disclaim any liability to any party for any loss, damage, or disruption caused by errors or omissions, whether such errors or omissions result from negligence, accident, or any other cause.

Content contained or made available through this book is not intended to and does not constitute legal advice or investment advice and no attorney-client relationship is formed. The publisher and the author are providing this book and its contents on an "as is" basis. Your use of the information in this book is at your own risk.

www.ExpertPress.net

Table of Contents

Disclosures 5

"Endorsements" 7

Introduction 9

Chapter 1
Sand Schmand 15

Chapter 2
It's Friday, but Sunday's Coming! 25

Chapter 3
I Thought I Wanted a Career;
It Turns Out All I Wanted Was a Paycheck 37

Chapter 4
Fifty Bucks Says I Don't Have a Gambling Problem 45

Chapter 5
The Eighth Wonder of the World? 51

Chapter 6
The Fine Line Between Taking a Calculated Risk
and Doing Something Stupid 63

Chapter 7
And I Thought IRAs and 401(k)s Were a Good Thing 77

Chapter 8
Do I Need Professional Help? 85

Chapter 9
Is It Time to Defund? 93

Chapter 10
Don't Worry, Be Happy 107

Chapter 11
How to Maximize Your Social Security in One Easy Step 111

Chapter 12
Sorry, I Forgot My Wallet 119

Chapter 13
Let's Not Jump to Conclusions 127

About the Author 129

Even More About the Author 131

Disclosures

Derek Colton offers investment advisory services through Aegis Wealth Management. The firm is registered as an investment advisor with the Securities and Exchange Commission (SEC) and only conducts business in states where it is properly registered or is excluded from registration requirements. Registration is not an endorsement of the firm by securities regulators and does not mean the advisor has achieved a specific level of skill or ability.

Neither the publisher nor the author shall be liable for damages arising here from and specifically disclaim any liability, loss, or risk taken by individuals who directly or indirectly act on the information contained herein. While every effort has been made to make this book as complete and accurate as possible, there may be mistakes, both typographical and in content. Use at your own risk.

All expressions of opinion are subject to change. You should consult with a professional advisor before implementing any of the strategies discussed. Content should not be viewed as an offer to buy or sell any securities or products mentioned. Tax information provided is general in nature and should not be construed as legal or tax advice. Always consult an attorney or tax professional regarding your specific legal or tax situation. Tax laws, as well as Social Security rules and regulations, are subject to change at any time.

Different types of investments and products involve higher and lower levels of risk. There is no guarantee that a specific investment or strategy will be suitable or profitable for an investor's portfolio. There are no assurances that a portfolio will match or exceed any particular benchmark. All investment strategies have the potential for profit or loss. Asset allocation and diversification do not ensure or guarantee better performance and cannot eliminate the risk of investment losses.

Projections are based on assumptions that may not come to pass. They do not reflect the impact that advisory fees and other investment-related expenses will have on the value of an investor's portfolio.

All insurance products are subject to the claims-paying ability of the insurer.

"Endorsements"

"This is the most wonderful book ever, written by a very handsome young man."

Derek's mother, who doesn't see very well

"This book reveals the unfortunate truth about Mr. Colton; he inexplicably and unfortunately expects people to care for themselves."

An anonymous politician serving his 37th term

"This book is stupendous, phenomenal, perfect, the best book ever, and everybody agrees with me."

An anonymous resident of 1600 Pennsylvania Avenue

"I love money. I love everything about it. I bought some pretty good stuff. Got me a $300 pair of socks. Got a fur sink. An electric dog polisher. A gasoline-powered turtleneck sweater. And, of course, I bought some dumb stuff, too."

— Steve Martin

*"Honor the Lord with your wealth,
with the firstfruits of all your crops."*

Proverbs 3:9

Introduction

With This Teeny Tiny Ring, I Thee Wed

I got my first job as a paperboy in Cedar Rapids, Iowa, at the age of 12. If you must have a paper route, Iowa is not the place to do it. I clearly remember riding my bike (or attempting to) in a foot or more of snow with below-zero temperatures and wind-chills of minus 25 or worse. Is it any wonder I grew to absolutely HATE the cold?

There were times when my dad would get up in the middle of the night and help me. He'd ride along in the car and fold and band the papers as I took them to the houses. This amazes me to this day. Just a very, very good man. Even more remarkable is that I was the fifth child, the fourth to have a paper route, and he still found time to help me!

But, even with his occasional assistance, I was a horrible paperboy and businessman. If a particular customer's house were a bit inconvenient to get to, I did what any hardworking, industrious young man would do: I skipped them. I was constantly late, and for the life of me, I could not seem to stay off old man Sinclair's front lawn (something he reminded me about regularly).

In those days, we had to go around on Friday evenings and collect money from our customers for the previous week's papers. This was known as "collecting," and I didn't like it. Why not? First of all, on Friday nights, both "The Brady Bunch" and "The

Partridge Family" were on. And since there were no DVRs or even VCRs in those days, I HAD to watch it live.

The other reason I hated collecting was that I had some clients who would be MIA when I would come to collect, sometimes for many weeks in a row. I was fairly sure some of these less-than-upstanding customers were actually home, as I heard them talking behind their closed front doors. They just didn't want to face the music of their enormous outstanding balance. When I would finally catch them, they might be three or four weeks behind, and I had to ask them for upward of $3. (I know what you're thinking — yeah, but $3 was a lot back then.) Actually, it's not a lot now and wasn't much then either. These people just didn't want to pay. Anyway, trying to collect "all" that money at once did not sit well with them, and some of these high-class customers would yell and swear at me.

My solution? Stop collecting all together but continue delivering the papers. Great business decision. It all came crashing down when the circulation manager showed up at our house and announced to my parents that I owed the newspaper $108! Of course, I did not have the $108, so it fell on my parents. They must have been so proud. In essence, they were buying the newspapers for the entire neighborhood and were unwitting philanthropists. I'm still not sure where they got the $108, but I suspect it was paid in installments, probably over 10 years or so! Not surprisingly, my paperboy career came to an abrupt halt.

During my freshman year in college, I am proud to say that I accumulated one of the finest collections of music albums anywhere on the third floor of Burge dormitory: The Partridge Family, Michael Jackson, Stevie Wonder, Madonna, nothing but the best. All courtesy of my student loan money. Wait. What? You're supposed to use your student loans for tuition, books, and room and board? I swear, nobody ever mentioned that to me. Must've been in the fine print somewhere. Guess what happens when you attend classes but don't use your student loan to pay your tuition? Well, they let you go right ahead and go to class but then give you no credit for it. The nerve! I diligently (sort of) attended classes for an entire semester, turned in all — and when I say all, I mean very few — of my assignments, took the final exams, and accumulated zero credit hours. They had quite a racket going.

Fast-forward a few years to my next venture, buying mobile homes and renting them out to my college buddies. Surprisingly, my friends, in fact, paid their rent, which I proceeded to spend on beer, girls, and Pac-Man. The latter was not a total waste; I was the (self-proclaimed) Sit-Down Pac-Man champion at Joe's Place in Iowa City for many years. I have no doubt that many of those records stand to this day. It's amazing how proficient you can get at video games if you skip most of your classes. The problem with this well-thought-out business plan was that even though my buddies paid me their rent, I had no money left after my indulgences to spend on luxuries like lot rent and utilities for the mobile homes. I think we call this poor money management. Psychologists call it "failure to launch" — a fancy way of saying you're a loser.

There are other stories of financial malfeasance as well. Like when my 1973 Pinto with a broken leaf spring and no reverse got repossessed. I'm not quite sure why the bank even wanted it back. But banks can be funny that way. Not too long after that, my fiancée's engagement ring was repo'd. To say it was repo'd is a bit of poetic license. The fact of the matter was, the big beautiful diamond I initially proposed with, which she proceeded to show off to the entire world, came with monthly payments that were much too high ... since I really couldn't afford ANY payments!

Can you imagine asking your fiancée for her ring back so you could replace it with one that had a diamond the size of a grain of sand? I had some explaining to do to her family as to why she no longer had the original ring. Your memory has an innate ability to block out traumatic experiences, so I have no recollection of how that conversation went, but I'm sure I was quite creative. I have absolutely no idea why she went ahead and married me. The woman is just a saint, plain and simple!

There was also my initial dabbling in the stock market and other investments, which lost me tens of thousands of dollars of borrowed money. It didn't occur to me before it was much too late that borrowing money for a highly speculative investment like the stock market might not be a great plan. Also, as a young man, I didn't take advantage of my employer's match to my 401(k). Huge mistake, especially when you're young, as you miss out on the miracle of compound interest. And I consistently violated the cardinal rule of responsible money management: SPEND LESS THAN YOU MAKE! Such a simple concept, but it somehow escaped me. I could go on, but I think you probably get the idea. I was not exactly a financial mastermind.

You may be wondering why I am telling you about all of these, shall we say ... missteps? I want you to understand that I do not come at this retirement planning thing from a position of arrogance or condescension. Any mistake you may have made along the way when it comes to your finances, I have also made (and probably times a factor of 10). But, if you believe, as I do, that our greatest lessons come from our biggest failures, then I have learned A LOT of great lessons along the way.

By His grace, God has enabled me to take those lamentable experiences and use them for the benefit of others, including, of course, my clients.

In the chapters ahead, we will be discussing the specifics of various aspects of retirement planning — which, by the way, is typically considered a very dry subject, right up there with the topic of my next book, "The Fascinating History of Rice Cakes at Actuarial Conventions." But I've done my best to make it at least somewhat entertaining. As long as we're on the subject, a few words about my sense of humor, I've been told that "it just ain't right," so proceed at your own risk.

One more thing. Keep in mind that all seven of you who read this book will be in completely different situations. For that reason, I can only go into so much detail. The bottom line is this: In order for us to move beyond generalities, we will need to get together for a free consultation where we can really dive into the specifics of your situation. Let's say you went to your doctor and he diagnosed you with a severe case of sphenopalatine ganglioneuralgia. Before you took any curative measures, you might want a second opinion, right? Well, think of the free consultation as nothing more than a second opinion on your current retirement plan, or lack thereof. No pressure, no commitments, and, of course, no charge. By the way, sphenopalatine ganglioneuralgia is doctor speak for brain freeze. So slow down on that double fudge, mint chocolate chip cookie dough ice cream, and you'll probably be just fine.

I'm no genius, as you'll soon discover, but it seems to me that based on the above criteria, you have nothing to lose by following in the footsteps of hundreds and hundreds of others and scheduling a meeting with us. Oh, did I mention it's free?

OK. Enough of this meaningless chatter. Let's get into it ...

"Money is better than poverty, if only for financial reasons."

— Woody Allen

"Honor the Lord with your wealth and with the firstfruits of all your produce; then your barns will be filled with plenty, and your vats will be bursting with wine."

Proverbs 3:9-10

Chapter 1

Sand Schmand

My clients come from a variety of sources. They may have heard my radio show or been referred by an existing client. We also regularly conduct estate planning workshops at various venues around the metro area. Many of those who attend the workshops will ultimately come into our offices and meet with our estate planning attorney to have their trust drawn up.

After the trust is executed, I, as a financial advisor, walk these folks through the process of funding their trust. Often these trust clients also need guidance with retirement planning, which, of course, is where yours truly comes in.

And then there are my groupies who show up at our offices just to get a picture with me or get my autograph. Actually, I'm still waiting for this to happen, but I'm almost 60, and time is running out.

My clients typically range in age from their early 50s through 80 years old and up. People in this age range are either close to retirement or in retirement, and they are at the critical stage to make these decisions and implement a plan of action.

Anyway, all of that is just a long-winded way of saying that my clients come to me from all walks of life, from various sources, and for many different reasons. But, in the end, all of this leads to my specialty — retirement planning.

There is one commonality among my clients, however: their humility and desire for input.

A while back, my wife and I were on vacation in Florida. One day, we went for a drive in our "midsize" rental car (which in rental car agency language means microscopic), and we came across one of the spectacular white sand beaches in the area. Being ignorant of the hazards of driving a tiny two-wheel-drive car on the sand, I told my wife I thought it would be a cool idea to drive onto the beach, closer to the water. She then pointed out to me that the other vehicles on the beach, with no exception, were four-wheel-drive trucks, and maybe driving this particular vehicle on the sand wasn't such a great idea.

I responded with something like, "Oh, sand schmand. How hard can it be?" Well, as it turned out, it wasn't hard — it was impossible! We were fender deep in soft, albeit beautiful, Florida sand inside of 30 seconds. Fortunately, the beach was full of well-tanned, muscle-bound, good Samaritans who helped us out. These locals with their four-wheel-drive vehicles obviously understood the challenges of driving on the sand. But rather than follow their example (or listen to my wife), in my arrogance, I decided that I knew better.

Here's the thing, the folks that become my clients are thirsty for guidance, direction, and counsel. They have left any tendency to "know it all" at the door and understand that arrogance has no place when it comes to making some of the most important decisions of their lives. This attitude of humility is the one thing my clients have in common, and it serves them very well when it comes to retirement planning and many other things, such as driving on the sand!

When we meet, we'll start a process that is aimed at answering three questions: Where are you? Where do you want to go? And lastly, how are you going to get there?

I liken this to planning a trip. If you want to get from point A to point B, the first thing you need to know is your starting point. Then, of course, you'll need to determine where you are going. And finally, you'll need to decide how you are going to get there.

I like to call our first consultation the "*Where are you?*" meeting, and it is basically an assessment of your current situation. I'll be asking you some pertinent questions, such as:

- How much do you have in retirement savings?
- What types of investments are we talking about? Stocks? Mutual funds? Bonds? Certificates of deposit (CDs)? Annuities? Real estate?
- What is your current income from all sources?
- What are your living expenses?
- What are your debts?
- How much income will you need from your investments, and when will you need it?
- Have you started Social Security? How much is it?
- If you haven't started Social Security, when do you plan to start it?
- When will you retire?
- Is it important for you to leave a portion of your estate to your heirs?
- Do you have a trust? Is it up to date?
- Do you have life insurance? How much?

- Do you have long-term care coverage?
- What is it about your current plan or advisor that you like/don't like?
- What are the fees on your investments?
- What would you consider to be a reasonable return on your investments?
- What are your criteria for making a change to your investment strategies or your advisor?

And the second most important question I ask at this point is this: *What is it you want this money to do for you?* Is it to live on? Is it to accumulate to obscene levels? Is it specifically for long-term care expenses? Do you want to leave a legacy? To what degree do you want to intervene financially in the lives of your children and grandchildren? And so on.

What I'm doing here is trying to gather enough information so that I have a complete understanding of your current situation. Only then can we move forward to steps two and three.

Typically, at this point, if a prospective client desires, I will collect their current investment statements and do an in-depth analysis of the returns, fees, risks, etc.

Occasionally, prospective clients who are not crazy about being forthcoming with their current investments or financial situation show up. They think we are negotiating the price on a used Ford pickup or something, and they want to hear my proposal before they share anything with me.

Roger was a perfect example. In doing my information gathering, it became clear that he did not want to divulge much about his current investments or investment strategy. How did I know this? He said so! His remarks were something to the effect of, "I want to know what you have to offer and what your recommendations would be before I get into all the details of my situation."

So, I asked him, "Roger, what would happen if you went to your doctor tomorrow and said, 'I don't feel well. Please prescribe something for me.' What would he do?" Roger looked a bit confused and said, "He wouldn't prescribe anything without knowing what was wrong with me." To which I said, "BINGO!" Unless your doctor mentored under Jack Kevorkian, he would refuse to prescribe anything until he got the answers to some important questions: Where does it hurt? What are the symptoms? How long has it been going on? He'll then proceed to take your blood pressure, listen to your heart, and probably get your weight (I hate that part).

The point is, he cannot give you a potential cure without a diagnosis, and he can't make a diagnosis without your cooperation and input. Retirement planning is the same way. Dr. Colton (I'm sure you've guessed by now that I'm not an actual medical doctor) cannot help you decide where to go until he knows where you are.

So, when you come in, don't be like Roger. Please be prepared to answer some basic questions about your current situation. I promise, I won't weigh you!

One more quick point on this subject, I am a fiduciary, which means I have a legal obligation to act in YOUR best interest. How can I possibly know what that is if I don't know anything about you? More on that later.

The next step in retirement planning answers the question: *Where are you going?*

This second step begins where the first one left off, with a review of my analysis of your current investment accounts. This review can be critically important. I believe that one of the most important responsibilities I have as a retirement planner is to make sure that what you want to do with your retirement savings is, in fact, what you ARE doing. So often, I find an incongruence between these two issues as with the following clients:

Suzanne told me she didn't want to lose ANY of her retirement money, yet nearly all of it was invested in small-cap stocks. Huh? That's like saying you want to lose weight, but your diet consists of nothing but beer and ice cream — something I've attempted by the way. It doesn't work. Maybe if I tried it with light beer?

The Thompsons insisted that they needed to lower their management fees, yet they were considering a variable annuity (VA). More on this topic later, but VA fees can be over 4%. Sign me up!

Vince and Carol's only objective was to leave money to their kids. Yet they had never been introduced to the concept of a gift trust, which would allow for a tax-free legacy to be left to their heirs.

These are but a few of the well-intentioned but misinformed or misguided folks I regularly come across, people with a discrepancy between what they want to do or think they are doing and what they are actually doing. Usually, these are not insurmountable issues to resolve, but first, they need to be uncovered, most of which is done by a thorough analysis of your current investments compared to the answers you provided in step one.

Step two is also where we talk about things like your risk tolerance. How much of the money that you have saved are you willing to lose in an attempt to get a better return? If the answer is none, you might want to reconsider that surefire investment — paying 37% a year, mind you — in the oceanfront condos in Guthrie, Oklahoma. Seriously though, risk tolerance is an all-important facet of retirement planning.

So what exactly determines your risk tolerance? Well, first would be your age. I often tell my clients that if you are 65 and investing as though you are 35, you are either really brave, really rich, or really dumb. Your timeline also has a lot to do with your risk tolerance. The question here is how soon, if ever, do you need your money? If you are 60 but do not need your retirement funds until age 70, you can afford to take more risk than if you need those funds next week!

The first time I met with Bob and Nancy, they told me with great enthusiasm that they were going on an around-the-world cruise in a few months. It was going to cost upward of $200,000, which they currently had invested in equities. After my chest pains subsided, I stressed to them that with these funds being needed in the (very) short term, they should probably be invested in something safe and easily accessible like a money market account rather than having the money at risk in the market.

Another determinate of your risk tolerance is your ability to withstand the emotions that can come with investment volatility. If you curl up in the fetal position every time you lose a few hundred bucks, clearly, you need a very conservative investment mix. (You might also need to be institutionalized. For more on that, pick up a copy of my last book, "Do I Need to Be Institutionalized?")

I simplify the risk tolerance issue by using a short questionnaire that will come up with a number between one and 100, based on the answers you provide. A score of one means that you want a portfolio with no risk, whereas a score of 100 is the equivalent of putting all your worldly possessions on black (or red, if you prefer) and spinning the roulette wheel.

So, we've answered, *Where are you?* and *Where are you going?* Now, step three is: *How are you going to get there?*

Step three is the point in the planning process in which we determine the specific investment vehicles that will help you get to where you want to go, at a risk level that is acceptable to you.

These investments can run the gamut from CDs to stocks to exchange-traded funds and dozens of others.

We need to put our heads together to figure out how you can best hang on to what you have, so you can use your retirement savings for the things you want — when you want them. Advisor Nick Murray tells his clients, "You've won the war. Now it's my job to help you negotiate the peace treaty" — meaning that you've worked your entire life to accumulate this money, and now it's his job to help you figure out how to hang on to it and put it to work for you in a way that enables you to sleep at night.

Speaking of sleeping at night, I like to use the acronym SWAN when describing the retirement plan we put together for you. Though it's a bit corny, SWAN stands for <u>S</u>leep <u>W</u>ell <u>at</u> <u>N</u>ight. (I told you it was corny.) But it accurately describes my objective as your retirement planner. John, one of my newer and more colorful clients, took this SWAN concept to another level and turned it into a verb. After we implemented his new retirement plan, he said, "Finally, I'm swanning!"

Beyond investment vehicles, the *How are you going to get there?* step covers things like the establishment of a gift trust or perhaps a charitable remainder trust that you may need to consider if the situation calls for it. By the way, if you have significant funds that you want to be sure are passed on to a charity, or if you have a specific amount in mind that you want to leave to certain heirs, your advisor should have talked to you about the trusts I've mentioned. If they haven't, they should be forced to sit and watch all 37 seasons of "Keeping Up With the Kardashians" back to back. Or you could just de-employ them, which might be a more humane way to go.

Where are you? Where do you want to go? How are you going to get there? The answers to the questions will help form the basis on which we put together your retirement plan.

By the way, I forgot to mention the most critical question I ask when gathering your information during the *Where are you?* step: *Do you have any dieting secrets you can share with me?*

"The best way to teach your kids about taxes is to eat 40% of their ice cream."

— Billy Crystal

"For where your treasure is, there your heart will be also."

Matthew 6:21

Chapter 2

It's Friday, but Sunday's Coming!

Unlike generic financial planning, effective retirement planning must address risks that are unique to retirees. These risks include market risk, longevity risk, interest rate risk, the sequence of returns risk, and black swan events, among others. While these subjects do need to be addressed with any type of financial planning, they take on more significance leading up to and during your retirement years.

Let's take a closer look at each of these and how we eliminate or, at the very least, mitigate them.

Inflation Risk

As I write this, inflation is about 2.5%, which doesn't really sound like much, does it? Well, it's not if you don't plan to live long. But look at the chart on the next page:

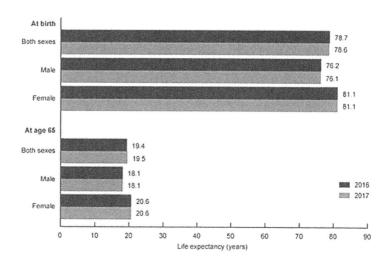

Source: NCHS, National Vital Statistics System, Mortality

Interesting, right? This chart shows that even though life expectancy at birth is around 79, if you make it to 65, you are expected to live another 19 years! If my math is correct, that puts you at age 84. A 65-year-old couple has a 50% chance that one of them (usually the Mrs.) will live until age 92 and a 25% chance that one of them (again, usually the Mrs.) will live to age 97. The point is, you can live an exceptionally long time after retirement, making that 2.5% inflation number enormous.

Incidentally, if you're wondering about the real reason women live longer than men, here you go:

Source: **boredpanda.com**

Source: **reddit.com**

You'll be relieved to know that yours truly is not depicted in either of those photos.

Back to the subject at hand: 2.5% inflation means an item that costs $1 today will cost $1.85 in 25 years. For the retiree, this means that maintaining your retirement income over the length of your retirement won't cut it. Your retirement income must go UP substantially to buy the current equivalent of goods and services in 25 years. The question then becomes — how exactly do we accomplish this?

I'll discuss this topic periodically throughout the coming chapters, but basically, we achieve this goal by aggressively limiting your investment losses while maximizing your gains. Unless you are uber wealthy, in retirement, you simply cannot afford to subject your portfolio to large losses. On the other hand, if you invest everything in 1% CDs, it means your purchasing power will actually be decreasing by 1.5% every year when inflation is taken into consideration. The trick here is to find a balance between safety and growth, and I, your trusty advisor, will show you how to do exactly that when we meet!

Market Risk

Again, this will be discussed in more detail in the next few chapters, but according to Investopedia, market risk is "the possibility of an investor experiencing losses due to factors that affect the overall performance of the financial markets in which he or she is involved."

The chart below demonstrates how devastating market risk can be:

If you lose:	Gain required to break even:
10%	11.11%
20%	25.00%
30%	42.86%
40%	66.67%
50%	100.00%
75%	300.00%
90%	900.00%

Source: Boston Charts Technical Analysis

So, if you have $100,000 and lose 50% (which many folks did in 2008), you're down to $50,000. Gain the same 50% back, and you're only at $75,000.

Sort of hard to fathom (at least for someone of my limited intellect), but somehow, it takes a 100% gain to make up for a 50% loss. Weird right?

The solution? DON'T LOSE 50% IN THE FIRST PLACE! I'll show you how to do precisely that in the next chapter.

One side note on this funny math: If you have a 50% loss, followed by a 50% gain, your return should be zero, right? But in the example above, was your return zero? No, it was not. It was -25%! Be very careful when you start hearing about "average" returns, as they may not be what they appear to be.

Let's talk for just a minute about the effect a bear market can have on your retirement outlook. A bear market is defined as a decline of 20% or more in stock prices over a period of two months or more. As you can see in the chart below, it can sometimes take years to recover from bear markets:

A History of S&P 500 Bear Markets

Peak	Trough	Drawdown	# of Days
9/7/1929	6/1/1932	-86.2%	998
9/7/1932	2/27/1933	-40.6%	173
7/18/1933	10/21/1933	-29.8%	95
2/6/1934	3/14/1935	-31.8%	401
3/6/1937	3/31/1938	-54.5%	390
11/9/1938	4/8/1939	-26.2%	150
10/25/1939	6/10/1940	-31.9%	229
11/9/1940	4/28/1942	-34.5%	535
5/29/1946	10/9/1946	-26.6%	133
6/15/1948	6/13/1949	-20.6%	363
7/15/1957	10/22/1957	-20.7%	99
12/12/1961	6/26/1962	-28.0%	196
2/9/1966	10/7/1966	-22.2%	240
11/29/1968	5/26/1970	-36.1%	543
1/11/1973	10/3/1974	-48.2%	630
9/21/1976	3/6/1978	-19.4%	531
11/28/1980	8/12/1982	-27.1%	622
8/25/1987	12/4/1987	-33.5%	101
7/16/1990	10/11/1990	-19.9%	87
7/17/1998	8/31/1998	-19.3%	45
3/24/2000	10/9/2002	-49.1%	929
10/9/2007	3/9/2009	-56.8%	517
4/29/2011	10/3/2011	-19.4%	157
9/20/2018	12/24/2018	-19.8%	95

Source: awealthofcommonsense.com

Here's how Bloomberg characterizes bear markets: "So the average bear market lasts about 14 months and takes about 25 months from which to recover — IF NO WITHDRAWALS ARE MADE! With life expectancy being what it is, the average retiree will face three bear markets during their retirement years. So clearly, if the potential effect of these bear markets is not mitigated, it could spell disaster for your retirement portfolio and income." (Bloomberg Financial, January 2016)

Another risk strongly associated with market risk that needs to be dealt with in retirement planning is something called systematic risk.

Systematic Risk

Systematic risk is something that cannot be mitigated by diversification in the market because, as the word implies, it affects the entire market. So, you can be diversified all you like in large-, small-, and micro-cap stocks, mutual funds, etc. to no avail; you're going to lose money in a market downturn.

I'm sure you are asking, "What in the world am I supposed to do to protect my retirement funds from market and systematic risk?" Excellent question, and one that can be a great icebreaker when meeting new people — if you don't want any friends. While diversifying in various equities may not help when it comes to systematic risk, asset class diversification can help. So, rather than simply diversifying by being invested in many different equities, we diversify by investing in uncorrelated classes of investments. In addition to stocks, this may include bonds, real estate, or certain types of insurance or bank products. The idea is that just because the market drops, it does not necessarily mean the other classes of investments will also lose value. Got it? Good! While finding the ideal mix of asset classes can be daunting, I employ strategies that do that very thing!

Longevity Risk

While the term "longevity risk" seems as if it could be synonymous with the inflation and life expectancy risks that we discussed previously, it has more to do with designing your retirement portfolio to ensure you won't run out of income during your lifetime.

Basically, there are four ways to accomplish this goal: 1) die sooner (not a great option), 2) live on less money (also undesirable), 3) continue to work during retirement (also called not retiring), 4) start with more money or take steps to make certain that your income is coming from a guaranteed source, a strategy which we will discuss in the following chapters.

Interest Rate Risk

As of this writing, interest rates are some of the lowest in history. If you are getting a home loan or other type of financing, this can be a wonderful thing, but for the retiree wanting to produce income, it can be a real source of frustration. Remember when we could get 18% CDs or 6%-8% on our savings accounts? Walk into a bank now and ask for those kinds of rates, and the men in the white jackets will be summoned to take you away. On the flip side, you also would have paid 15% or 18% for your home mortgage back in those days.

The point is, if you're looking for fixed-rate investments like CDs to sustain you in retirement, well, good luck. Another issue with these low rates is that they are much more likely to go up than down, which creates yet another challenge. Retirees have depended on bonds for years, but they tend to lose value in a rising interest rate environment, which makes them much less appealing as a go-to source for retirement income.

The solution to interest rate risk is to use investments that are at least somewhat immune from interest rate volatility. Stay tuned for details!

Sequence of Returns Risk

The sequence of returns risk is the risk that you will have a substantial drop in your investment account value in the early years of your retirement. When this happens, it can drastically reduce the amount of income available for you during your retirement years. Worse yet, it could mean running out of money before you run out of life.

Take a look at the following chart:

SEQUENCE OF RETURNS RISK
Distribution Phase: $1,000,000 Beginning Balance

Age	Investor A			Investor B	
	Annual Return[1]	Portfolio Year-End Value[3]	Withdrawals	Annual Return[2]	Portfolio Year-End Value[3]
65	-9.03%	$844,700.00	($65,000.00)	13.48%	$1,069,800.00
66	-11.85%	$679,603.05	($65,000.00)	31.15%	$1,338,042.70
67	-21.97%	$465,294.26	($65,000.00)	15.89%	$1,485,657.69
68	28.36%	$532,251.71	($65,000.00)	2.10%	$1,451,856.50
69	10.74%	$524,415.55	($65,000.00)	14.82%	$1,602,021.63
70	4.83%	$484,744.82	($65,000.00)	25.94%	$1,952,586.04
71	15.61%	$495,413.48	($65,000.00)	-36.55%	$1,173,915.84
72	5.48%	$457,562.14	($65,000.00)	5.48%	$1,173,246.43
73	-36.55%	$225,323.18	($65,000.00)	15.61%	$1,291,390.20
74	25.94%	$218,772.01	($65,000.00)	4.83%	$1,288,764.34
75	14.82%	$186,194.02	($65,000.00)	10.74%	$1,362,177.64
76	2.10%	$125,104.10	($65,000.00)	28.36%	$1,683,491.21
77	15.89%	$79,983.14	($65,000.00)	-21.97%	$1,248,628.19
78	31.15%	$39,897.89	($65,000.00)	-11.85%	$1,035,665.75
79	13.48%	-$19,723.88	($65,000.00)	-9.03%	$877,145.13
	5.93%	Arithmetic Average[4]		5.93%	
	4.14%	Geometric Average[5]		4.14%	

[1] S&P 500 dividend reinvested returns from 2000 to 2014 (DOES NOT include deductions for investment fees)

Source: http://pages.stern.nyu.edu/~adamodar/New_Home_Page/datafile/histretSP.html

I find this absolutely fascinating. Investor A and Investor B both start with $1 million in retirement funds. Both live on the $65,000 a year they take out of their accounts. Yet, you'll notice that at age 79, Investor A has run out of money while Investor B still has $877,000. This really doesn't seem to add up since both started with the same amount of money, both started at the same age, and both withdrew $65,000 each year from their accounts.

Furthermore, you'll notice that the average returns on their accounts are identical, both 5.93%. The only difference is the sequence of those returns. We call this, duh, the sequence of returns risk, yet another risk that retirees can face. If you look closely, you'll notice that the returns on this chart are simply reversed. Whereas Investor A started with a -9.03% return the first year and ended with a 13.48% return in the last year, Investor B began with a 13.48% return and finished up with -9.03% return.

Significant losses in the early years of a retirement portfolio can have a devastating effect on everything that follows, even to the point of running out of money. But experience positive returns during those same years, and you're golden.

So, what's all this about? Here's the deal. Do you, or I, or anyone else know with any degree of certainty in what order those returns will come? If you think you do, you probably also thought the Titanic was unsinkable and O.J. was innocent.

Black Swan Events

The term "black swan" was popularized by finance professor and former Wall Street trader Nassim Taleb. Prior to the 16th century, there was no known account of swans with anything other than white feathers. That all changed, however, in 1697, when Dutch explorers discovered the existence of black swans in Western Australia. So, when Taleb applies this term to the financial markets, he is describing an unpredictable event, based on information available at the time. These events can cause catastrophic results to the financial markets, and, in turn, to your investments.

September 11, 2001, was just such an event, as was the COVID-19 pandemic, the housing meltdown in 2008, the dot-com meltdown in 2001, and the market crash in 1929.

These were all black swan events. No amount of financial acumen or extensive investment experience would have prevented most people from the dire consequences these events had on their traditional, market-based retirement accounts. The solution? A well-designed, retirement-friendly plan that is at least partially immune from such calamities. Fortunately, you are in good hands, as mitigating the potentially disastrous effects caused by black swan events is my specialty!

After reviewing this chapter, I feel as if I should talk to my doctor about upping the dosage of my antidepressants. But it also made me think of a sermon I heard many years ago by Tony Campolo. It was entitled, "It's Friday, but Sunday's Coming." Check it out on YouTube if you get the chance, as it contains a fantastic message. The crux of the sermon was that even though Good Friday was a very bleak day in the Christian faith because it was the day Christ was crucified, his followers didn't fully comprehend that there was reason for great hope! Why? Because Easter Sunday, the day it was discovered that Christ had been resurrected, was coming.

Granted, we are not talking about anything nearly as monumental as Good Friday and Easter. Still, this discouraging and seemingly hopeless chapter that details all the risks in dealing with retirement planning is the Friday. But Sunday's coming in the chapters ahead!

"I made my money the old-fashioned way. I was very nice to a wealthy relative right before he died."

— Malcolm Forbes

"How much better to get wisdom than gold, to get insight rather than silver!"

Proverbs 16:16

Chapter 3

I Thought I Wanted a Career; It Turns Out All I Wanted Was a Paycheck

When we put together a retirement plan for you, it is typically divided into two distinct parts. One part is the money you have set aside to live on, which is referred to as nondiscretionary spending. This money is typically used for everyday living expenses: housing, taxes, insurance, food, car maintenance, and the like. The other part is, you guessed it, money that you have set aside for discretionary spending on things like travel, new cars, a wine-glass holder necktie collection, or the air-conditioned pair of shoes you've always wanted.

Fellow author Tom Hegna brilliantly refers to this as paychecks and "playchecks." Since I'm not nearly as brilliant as Tom, we'll stick with nondiscretionary and discretionary. In this chapter, as the title so astutely implies, we will be talking about the characteristics of the investments used for your nondiscretionary spending.

The primary characteristic of these investments is that they must be dependable. Actually, I'm going to take it a step further by using a word that is typically frowned upon in financial planning circles — GUARANTEED. Yes, I said it. Your nondiscretionary income needs to be guaranteed. Why? Because I think you'd agree that going without food or housing in retirement, or anytime for that matter, is not an acceptable option.

The name of my company is Cornerstone Capital Management. I didn't just pick this name out of thin air.

By definition, a cornerstone is something that is essential, indispensable, or basic, the chief foundation on which something is constructed or developed.

For instance, the Bible tells us that Christ is the "Chief Cornerstone" of the Christian faith. He is the foundation on which Christians, like me, base their entire belief system. Without Christ as the cornerstone, there is no Christianity.

No doubt you've seen stories about those wacky people who build their houses on the edge of a cliff. Yes, it is a stunning view, but at what expense? Every several years, the rain comes, and the foundations of these homes begin to crumble. If owners are fortunate enough to get out in time, they are left with a stunning view — BUT NO HOUSE!

Well, the problem with these cliffside homes is that they were not built using a cornerstone or a foundation with any kind of stability. The results are not surprising. It's akin to having your nondiscretionary income streaming from insecure sources, such as the stock market. You never know when the rain may come, and that income source begins to crumble and fall off the proverbial cliff.

Remember the risks we discussed in the previous chapter? Investments that can generate guaranteed income are a must to mitigate those risks effectively. So, what income sources are we talking about when it comes to your nondiscretionary spending? Well, we start with things like Social Security and pensions. But here's the challenge; most people are not able to live on these two income sources alone. What this means then is we have to find a way to generate income from your retirement savings, IRAs, 401(k)s, TSPs, 403(b)s, brokerage accounts, and others.

One important point here: Some of my clients are in the enviable position of generating enough income from their pension, Social Security, etc., that they do not have to be concerned with income from their investments. If you are in such a position, congratulations; you are in rare company! What this means from a planning standpoint is that we can usually afford to take more risk with your investments and not be so concerned with safety, which we will discuss in an upcoming chapter.

More often, though, my clients are like Tim and Debbie, who came in to see me somewhat reluctantly. The couple was confident everything was in order with their retirement plan, but at Debbie's insistence, they came to me to be sure. They were quite surprised when I pointed out that their current plan was built on sand, with the majority of their money invested in equities and at risk. They had been lulled into a false sense of security built on the belief that even if the market goes down, it always comes back.

While that may be true, Tim and Debbie were 65, not 35. I pointed out to them that if we have a severe downturn, and the recovery takes many years, they will need to continue to withdraw funds from their account, making a recovery insufferably long, if not impossible. They might not get back to where they were. Worse yet, they could run out of money.

To further solidify my brilliant point, I showed them this chart, which we also talked about in the last chapter:

A History of S&P 500 Bear Markets

Peak	Trough	Drawdown	# of Days
9/7/1929	6/1/1932	-86.2%	998
9/7/1932	2/27/1933	-40.6%	173
7/18/1933	10/21/1933	-29.8%	95
2/6/1934	3/14/1935	-31.8%	401
3/6/1937	3/31/1938	-54.5%	390
11/9/1938	4/8/1939	-26.2%	150
10/25/1939	6/10/1940	-31.9%	229
11/9/1940	4/28/1942	-34.5%	535
5/29/1946	10/9/1946	-26.6%	133
6/15/1948	6/13/1949	-20.6%	363
7/15/1957	10/22/1957	-20.7%	99
12/12/1961	6/26/1962	-28.0%	196
2/9/1966	10/7/1966	-22.2%	240
11/29/1968	5/26/1970	-36.1%	543
1/11/1973	10/3/1974	-48.2%	630
9/21/1976	3/6/1978	-19.4%	531
11/28/1980	8/12/1982	-27.1%	622
8/25/1987	12/4/1987	-33.5%	101
7/16/1990	10/11/1990	-19.9%	87
7/17/1998	8/31/1998	-19.3%	45
3/24/2000	10/9/2002	-49.1%	929
10/9/2007	3/9/2009	-56.8%	517
4/29/2011	10/3/2011	-19.4%	157
9/20/2018	12/24/2018	-19.8%	95

Source: awealthofcommonsense.com

As I referred to the chart, I said, "Here's the thing, Tim and Debbie, these recovery times assume there are no deductions from your account to pay for food, clothing, housing, and other luxuries. When we factor those deductions into the equation, you will be facing the very real probability of running out of money."

Then I asked them, "How long would you like your money to last?"

They looked at each other for a second, and Tim replied, "For as long as we live?"

I said, "Good answer. How long will that be?"

"Oh, I don't know, maybe 20 or 25 years," Tim replied.

I asked, "With your current investment allocations, do you have any assurances that you won't outlive your money?"

Tim looked a bit confused and muttered something about the 4% rule. Or was it the 5% rule? For those of you who are not familiar with that term, the 4% or 5% rule (depending on who you ask) basically says that as long as you do not take more than 4% or 5% from your investments per year, you'll never run out of money because, in theory at least, the market will always return more than the 4% or 5% you are spending.

Unfortunately, many (dare I say most) in my industry put together retirement plans for their clients with no regard whatsoever to guarantees.

These well-intentioned (I think) advisors may say things like 1) if you want guarantees, you won't get any kind of return, 2) don't worry, the market always bounces back, or 3) it's only a paper loss. Perhaps these advisors are just uneducated or misinformed. Whatever the case, I believe they do the vast majority of retirees a disservice when they put together plans without guarantees of any kind, especially for clients who are depending on generating income from those investments.

Another argument I often hear from clients is that their advisor said they don't need guarantees because their investments can only go down so far with stop losses in place. I usually respond with a much kinder version of something like, "Seriously, you're falling for that bamboozlement?"

A stop loss is a trading strategy that, in theory, automatically sells you out of a particular investment, usually stocks, if it reaches a certain level. For instance, if you purchased IBM at $125, you could place a stop that would (again, in theory) automatically liquidate your position if it fell below a specific price point, say $115. This approach would hold your losses (still, in theory) to no more than $10 on the position.

However, there are notable exceptions to this strategy working as designed. September 11, 2001, was a Tuesday. When the first plane hit the World Trade Center at 8:45 a.m., the New York Stock Exchange had not yet opened. And guess what? It stayed closed until the following Monday. That's right, no stock trading of any kind for four business days. When the market finally opened, the NYSE was down 684 points, the largest single-day drop in history at that time. By the end of that week, it had lost 14%. Ouch.

But no worry, you say, because you had stop losses in place. Oh, really? Unless they were set up with limits (a more sophisticated strategy that I won't delve into at this point, since you may already be nodding off), those stop losses would not have done any good at all. As a matter of fact, those stop losses likely would have been executed at the open of the market on Monday, September 17, thereby all but ENSURING a substantial loss.

I have no way of knowing if you understood any of that — after reading it, I'm not sure I understood it — so let me put it more succinctly. Do not be lulled into a false sense of security because of a sometimes-effective-but-too-often-feeble strategy like stop losses to protect your life savings.

More than once, I have gotten into discussions with the soon-to-be ex-advisor of one of my new clients. On rare occasions, communication with this person is necessary to facilitate the transfer of the client's account to my firm. Invariably, if the client is also on the phone, this discussion leads to the former advisor extolling the virtues of the perfect plan he put together for the client.

The other advisor (not his real name) will usually say things like:

- "My client has averaged 112% year."
- "My fee is the lowest in town."
- "This plan was put together using the latest and greatest investment software and algorithms the world has ever seen or will see."
- "We have a relationship going back 75 years" (or some crazy thing).

The ex-advisor may even throw in, "I'm young, trim, and good looking. You, Mr. Colton, are none of those things." (I must admit, I have no comeback for that one.)

After I wipe the tears from my eyes, I ask one question. "So, Mr. ex-advisor, what assurances can you offer these former clients of yours that they will never run out of money?"

At that point, I usually hear, well, crickets. This person cannot and has not offered assurances of any kind. The entire plan he put together for the clients was developed upon assumptions and hypotheticals. This advisor and others like him have built their client's retirement plans on the edge of a cliff above Lake Arcadia. Please do not email me saying there are no cliffs at Lake Arcadia — I'm well aware — but I had to come up with something you could relate to!

If you are like Tim and Debbie, who I mentioned earlier in this chapter, you are hopefully beginning to understand why your nondiscretionary income needs to come from guaranteed sources. If you are still a doubter, please reread this chapter as many times as it takes for you to fall in line! In the next chapter, we will be discussing what types of vehicles we can use to generate your "paycheck."

"Economists report that a college education adds many thousands of dollars to a man's lifetime income — which he then spends sending his son to college."

— Bill Vaughn

"His master replied, 'Well done, good and faithful servant! You have been faithful with a few things; I will put you in charge of many things. Come and share your master's happiness!'"

Mathew 25:21

Chapter 4

Fifty Bucks Says I Don't Have a Gambling Problem

So, let's look at some of the options for income that involve guarantees. Essentially, there are three choices:

- Bank products that qualify for protection under the Federal Deposit Insurance Corporation (FDIC)
- U.S. Treasuries
- Fixed-rate (and indexed) annuities, which are guaranteed by the claims-paying ability of the insurance company and may be further guaranteed under state guaranty funds

Bank Products

Following the financial calamity of the late 1920s and early 1930s, the federal government enacted the Banking Act of 1933, which formed the FDIC.

As a result, your accounts at an FDIC member bank are insured up to $250,000. You can, in effect, raise this $250,000 limit by having different types of accounts at the same bank or accounts at several different banks.

Probably the most widely used bank investment for retirement accounts is a certificate of deposit. As I am writing this, five-year CDs are paying around 2.2%. The problem is that the inflation rate is about 2.5%, meaning you are netting a very generous -0.3% on your investment, which simply will not cut it over the length of your retirement.

There are, however, other types of CDs:

- Brokered CDs
- Callable CDs
- Market-linked or indexed CDs

The issue here is, no matter how you slice it, there is a better option than any type of CD, which we will discuss in the next chapter.

U.S. Treasuries

So, what about U.S. Treasuries? For the sake of our discussion, we are going to assume that we are talking about U.S. Treasury bonds. However, U.S. Treasuries also include things like Treasury bills and Treasury notes, which are basically shorter-term and lower-yielding versions of Treasury bonds.

When you buy a Treasury bond, you are actually loaning money to the U.S. government. I know you are shocked that our government would need a loan. Still, these bonds enable the government to pay for things such as $518,000 for studying the effects of cocaine on the sexual behavior of Japanese quail and $2,600,000 to train Chinese prostitutes to drink more responsibly on the job. I know what you're thinking, shouldn't we be spending that money on training AMERICAN prostitutes to drink more responsibly on the job before we reach out to the Chinese?

A 10-year Treasury bond, as of this writing, is paying an astounding 0.73%. Again, yes, it is guaranteed because the government can always print money if needed. But at 0.73%, a $10,000 investment will yield $73/year. Heck, that will barely buy you a poorly done mani-pedi. In case you're wondering, I do NOT know this from personal experience. But I do have a wife and five daughters who are quite knowledgeable on such critically important matters.

So, that leaves us with really only one decent guaranteed option, annuities.

Annuities

Daryl and his wife Maryanne came into my office a while back after hearing my radio show. One of the first things Daryl said was, "I don't like annuities, so you're wasting your time if that's one of the things you're going to talk to me about."

I said, "Oh, really? What is it you don't like about them?"

He responded with the typical comment I hear from clients who got their latest investment recommendation from their local barista, "They have high fees, the insurance company keeps your money when you die, and I can't get to my money if I need it."

Well, saying you do not like annuities is like saying you do not like food. The reality is — some food you like and other food you don't. Unless you're like me, I eat pretty much anything that's not green. The reasons Daryl came up with for not liking annuities are vast generalizations that may be true of some annuities but not of others. So, if you have a belief that tells you that ALL annuities are "bad," please hear me out for the next few pages while we explore this subject.

Where banks and government bonds can fetch you around next to nothing (plus or minus), a good annuity can average 5%-7% or more, generate guaranteed lifetime income, and even provide additional income in the event of nursing care.

The operative word in the previous sentence, however, is "good." As I alluded to, there are outstanding annuities and some that are, well, not so great. Let's talk about the latter first.

Variable Annuities

If you have one of these types of products, you have my condolences. Please call my office ASAP at 405-444-9067 to schedule an intervention.

The beauty of most annuities is that since your money is <u>not</u> invested in the market, you are not at risk of ever suffering a market loss. UNLESS that is, you have a variable annuity.

With VAs, your money <u>is</u> invested in the market, and your account can suffer very real losses, which, to my way of thinking, defeats the purpose of an annuity. In fairness, advocates for these products will tell you that though you can suffer losses to your investment account, variable annuities can still be designed with a guaranteed death benefit. Upon the annuity holder's death, their beneficiary will receive a payout of some predetermined amount. Of course, between now and your demise, your account could be seriously underwater or, in a worst-case scenario, depleted entirely (not my idea of sleeping well at night).

Another issue I have with the dreaded variable annuity is the frequent ridiculously high fee, which is almost always over 2%, usually around 3% or more. I have even seen some over 4%. (For those of you who voted for Gary Hart in the 1984 presidential primary, that means with a market return of say 6%, you would still net only 2% or 3% after subtracting the stupid fees, without accounting for inflation. Come to think of it, I think I may have voted for Gary Hart. But I was a naive 24-year-old whose brain was not fully developed, which may have been true of all of his supporters.)

Anyway, back to the point, variable annuities are not a guaranteed option as far as I'm concerned.

Immediate Annuities

Another type of annuity is the immediate annuity. This product takes a lump sum that you deposit and turns it into immediate income designed to last the rest of your life. These would be great if you KNEW you would live until you were 137 years old. The problem here is that upon you and your spouse's demise, any funds that may be remaining in the account could go poof. Meaning that if you and yours take a dirt nap in the short term, the insurance company is likely getting the better end of the deal.

Another issue with immediate annuities is that other than the income they generate, there are no funds available to you if you should need them for some reason. As the name implies, the money you deposit IMMEDIATELY belongs to the insurance company, and their only promise is to pay you an income. So, in my opinion, immediate annuities are not a desirable option as part of a retirement plan (except for rare occasions).

What about fixed annuities? They are definitely an option. As the name implies, these annuities pay a fixed interest rate for a specified period. Like a CD on steroids, five-year fixed annuities (as of this writing) are paying upward of 4%, almost double their bank counterparts. It's not a bad return, but is there an even better alternative for the guaranteed portion of your retirement funds?

So glad you asked. Enter the fixed-indexed annuity.

"Do you want to make money from Facebook? It's easy. Just go to your account settings, deactivate your account, and go to work."

— Anonymous

"Cast but a glance at riches, and they are gone, for they will surely sprout wings and fly off to the sky like an eagle."

Proverbs 23:5

Chapter 5

The Eighth Wonder of the World?

The Seven Wonders of the World, listed in the order of things I have heard of to others I didn't know existed until Googling are: The Great Wall of China, the Taj Mahal, Christ the Redeemer, the Roman Colosseum, and the cities of Petra, Chichen Itza, and Machu Picchu. Can we add the fixed-indexed annuity (FIA) as the eighth? Let's take a look.

In a nutshell, FIAs give you a portion of the upside when the market goes up, and, in exchange for surrendering some of the upside potential, you have no downside market risk. As a result, with a decent FIA, you can secure a higher return than with government bonds, money market accounts, or CDs while maintaining the safety aspect of those investments. Keep in mind here that FIAs, unlike VAs, aren't investing your money in the market. The market is simply used as a gauge to determine your performance. Thus, these products can deliver excellent upside performance with no downside market risk, which, to your humble author, makes it worth consideration for the eighth wonder of the world!

Since we all know a picture is worth a thousand words, please look at the chart below:

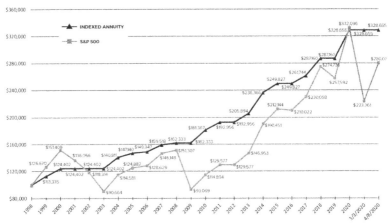

Source: Retirement Realized Agents Academy, LLC

The line marked with squares (and initially starting in the top position) is the S&P 500, and the line underneath marked with triangles is the FIA. A couple of assumptions in this example are 1) you began with $100,000 in 1998, and 2) this particular annuity is crediting you with half of the market upside.

You'll notice that when the S&P 500 goes up, the FIA goes up, albeit not quite as much. However, when the S&P 500 drops, what do you notice about the FIA? Right, it stays put. Now I will grant you that during the down-market years, the annuity does not go up in value, but the key here is that it does not go DOWN. As a result of having no downside over the long term — in this case, 20 years — the annuity actually outperforms the market despite the fact that you are only getting credited with half of the upside market performance.

Fixed-indexed annuities can be an ideal, retirement-friendly option. FIAs can help solve the issues of low interest rates, market volatility, and retirement income uncertainty, three of the major topics that need to be addressed when designing your retirement plan.

The first comment I usually get about this remarkable strategy is, "It sounds too good to be true." It's usually followed by, "How can they do that?"

Well, let me assure you, as hundreds of my clients would attest, it IS true. And since I would never expect any of my clients to invest in something that I wouldn't invest in, I can personally vouch for this approach. As I write this, we are in the middle of the hysteria surrounding the COVID-19 virus. The market is off about 25% from its high, meaning we are officially in a bear market. However, the FIAs that many of my clients own have not lost a penny!

When the market eventually recovers, these annuities will pick up right where they left off. No recovery is necessary since they never went down in the first place. Incidentally, I recently came across an indoor s'mores maker, which also sounds too good to be true, but it works!

Now, answering the "How can they do this?" question is another story. Do you want the long or the short answer? If you said the long answer, please call my office and schedule a meeting with me, after which we will rush you to the psych ward for an evaluation.

The short answer is, well, not that short. Insurance companies are required to invest the vast majority of their money in guaranteed investments, like U.S. government bonds. So, since their investments are guaranteed, they can pass those guarantees on to you. In other words, for the most part, nobody's money is actually invested in the market — not yours and not the insurance company's. Again, the market is just a determinate of performance.

So how does the insurance company make money? At the risk of you nodding off again, let me give this a shot. The insurance company takes a very small portion of the premium they receive and invests it in something called a derivative.

This particular derivative, also known as a call option, increases in value exponentially when the value of the index goes up. If the index goes up 10%, for example, the derivative might increase 100%, thus providing a nice profit to the insurance company, some of which they pass on to you, the annuity owner. In declining-market years, the insurance company does just fine; the vast majority of their investments are in accounts that will always bring in a profit.

I hope this answer to "How do they make money?" is sufficient, because now I'm nodding off. Again, when you come in for your initial consultation, I'll be happy to explain this until your heart's content — or until you start mumbling to yourself and drooling, whichever comes first.

In addition to decent upside potential with no downside risk, FIAs have numerous other compelling features.

First and foremost, FIAs can be designed to produce a guaranteed lifetime income. Regardless of how long you live or market performance, the annuity will provide income to you and your spouse (if a joint income option is selected), until both of you get stamped "return to sender." Unlike the immediate annuity, however, you are not surrendering your money to the insurance company when you begin your lifetime income. The money is still there, it is still yours, and it is still growing with the market index.

Compare this income feature to the previously mentioned 4% or 5% rule. If you recall, this rule assumes that you will never run out of income *if* the market returns as much or more than your withdrawals. My colleague Anthony Owen says it isn't income; it's *IFcome*. If the market does this, that, and the other, and if you die at a "reasonable age," you MIGHT have enough income to last your lifetime. Does that make you sleep well at night? If so, you may want to cut back on the Ambien.

Some FIAs can also be designed with a special provision that will increase your income (up to 100% in some cases) in the event you need in-home care or nursing care. An FIA of that type can potentially mitigate the need for expensive long-term care insurance policies.

And unlike the immediate annuity, when you and your spouse die, any funds left in the account are passed to your heirs, not relinquished to the insurance company.

One other huge plus with most annuities is that they grow tax-deferred, much like your individual retirement account (IRA) or 401(k). Take a look at the chart below that highlights the advantage of tax deferral:

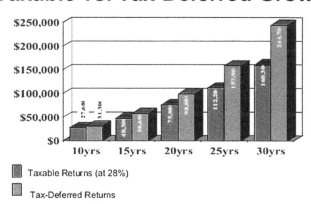

Source: Garman/Forgue, Personal Finance, Fifth Edition

So, we've touched on some of the highlights of FIAs, but I'm sure you are asking, "What is the downside?"

One downside is that typically the upside isn't what you might get with stock investments, at least in the short run. Remember, an FIA will usually give you a PORTION of the market's return, not all of it. Things like caps and participation rates can limit your upside. I won't get into this now; just keep in mind that your upside on FIAs will be limited to one degree or another. Having said that, one of the FIAs I use was up about 16% in 2019, and that is without downside market risk!

So, the question is: Would you be willing to give up a portion of your upside to have no downside market risk? Most retirees with both oars in the water and who are amenable to reason would answer, "Why yes, Mr. Colton, I'd take that deal any day."

Also, annuities have surrender periods accompanied by surrender charges. While most annuities allow for 10% withdrawals each year without any charges, you cannot think of this as your typical brokerage account or bank account where you can take money out willy-nilly. Annuities are a long-term proposition, usually between 7-10 years.

If you recall, the surrender charges on annuities stem from the fact that the issuing insurance company invests in long-term government bonds, among other things. If you decide to surrender your funds, the insurance company is forced to liquidate a portion of these bonds before their maturity date, costing them some of their investment return.

There are exceptions, however, to these surrender charges. With most FIAs, if either spouse dies, the surviving spouse could withdraw all the funds if they choose to, without any surrender charges. There can be similar exceptions for things like a terminal illness or certain types of nursing care.

I like to remind my clients of a brilliant point in regard to surrender charges on annuities as compared to brokerage accounts without surrender charges. If you started with, say, $500,000 in the stock market and your account is currently down 10%, and now you need to withdraw money, don't you, in effect, have a 10% surrender charge?

As ideal as FIAs can be for some investors, these types of accounts are by no means suitable for everyone. If you have relatively little in retirement savings, and you are withdrawing more than 5% or so of that money each year, an FIA may not be a good fit for you. Of course, having that money in the market probably isn't a good fit either. Should you find yourself in this situation, call my office, and we'll put our heads together and see if we can come up with a solution.

One more thing, while FIAs can typically be issued with no fees whatsoever, adding the lifetime income feature will usually require a charge of some kind, usually somewhere between 0.5% to 1% (or maybe more). Let me hasten to add, however, that unlike the fee you currently pay to your advisor who handles your brokerage account, an FIA fee gives you certain guarantees. Remind me again, what guarantees do you have with your current equity holdings? I thought so.

Steve and Carol came in to visit me after completing their trust with our estate planning attorney. Frankly, Carol had to twist Steve's arm even to set foot in my office. He had a long-term relationship with an advisor whom he thought had done a good job for him. And if we strictly look at the returns in his account, the advisor hadn't done too bad.

But after getting into more detail about their current investment strategy, it became clear some issues needed to be addressed. First of all, they were using the same investment strategies now as they had 20 years ago. They were invested in nearly all equities involving a high degree of risk. Their advisor had failed to consider their ages; Carol is in her mid-60s, and Steve was pushing 80 (or was it 180?). At any rate, he was much older than Carol.

Why is that important, you ask? As I mentioned earlier in this future best seller, a catastrophic market meltdown at this point in their lives would be, well, catastrophic. There is no time to "let the market come back." They were using those accounts for income now.

But here is the more critical point, with their age difference, it is highly likely that Carol will outlive Steve, possibly by a decade or more. By itself, that wouldn't be an issue if it were not for the fact that Steve "took care" of all the investment decisions. Carol had no clue what was going on with their retirement accounts, which was exactly why they were sitting in my office. She was understandably anxious about the possibility of Steve being past his sell-by date and leaving her to make investment decisions that she is not equipped to make.

I run into this scenario quite often. Widows whose husbands have passed are some of the more frequent callers to my radio show. Unfortunately, when their husbands die, many widows are left uninformed and bewildered about an appropriate course of action for their investments.

Back to Steve and Carol. After uncovering these issues, I proceeded to eloquently explain to them how a guaranteed account — in this case, an FIA — could go a long way toward easing Carol's angst.

I recommended taking a portion of the funds that were at risk in the market and moving them to an account that has no downside market risk. This strategy also produces LIFETIME income, thereby ensuring that Carol will never run out of money, regardless of the market, the economy, or President Trump's tweets. I like to refer to this as a seamless transition upon the passing of a spouse. There are no decisions or distress regarding investments; the income just keeps coming in.

Needless to say, Steve and Carol are "swanning" as we speak!

Let me hasten to make one more point regarding the importance of guaranteed accounts and my investment philosophy. Unlike some of the inferior advisors out there, I realize we are building a plan for YOUR money, not mine. Which, by extension, means that the decisions on how to invest your money are ultimately yours. I can make suggestions, give you advice and counsel, and try to steer you toward what I think you ought to do, but you may disagree with some of what I propose. (Then there are the engineers who disagree with EVERYTHING I propose.) Anyway, the plan we design is a joint effort. If you do not like the idea of giving up a portion of your upside to have no downside risk, that's absolutely fine; we adjust accordingly. If you like certain individual stocks or have an emotional attachment to your Sears stock, well, we can keep it. Now that I think about it, I'm not sure that one still exists, but you get the point.

Russ and Andrea were in my office not too long ago. The reason for their visit? Russ wanted to make some changes to some of his investments, and his soon-to-be ex-advisor said, "No." The advisor didn't say, "I wouldn't recommend it." He refused to go along with what his client wanted him to do. Huh? Somewhere along the line, this knuckleheaded advisor forgot that it isn't his money.

I want to design a sound retirement plan for you, one that is consistent with your goals and objectives and provides dignity and independence with no compromise in lifestyle. But I don't do this in a vacuum. You can provide as much or as little input as you wish, without ever having to be concerned about me forgetting that the money belongs to you. I really do not want the word "knucklehead" anywhere on my tombstone!

I'm often asked, "If an FIA is a good idea, why can't I just put all my money into those investments?" Well, there are several reasons.

The first of which is that "they" won't let you. Yes, big brother has stepped in and decided you are too stupid to know what is best for yourself. While that may actually be true for those who believe Elvis is still on tour, most of us are intelligent enough to figure out what is in our own best interest.

Nevertheless, as a result of industry imposed "guidelines," most insurance carriers that underwrite indexed annuities will not allow you to place more than 50%-75% of your liquid assets in an annuity.

Another reason I do not suggest putting all your retirement funds into guaranteed accounts is that these accounts typically are not entirely liquid. A portion of your money should be accessible on short notice without the imposition of surrender charges or penalties.

Also, keep in mind that while some indexed annuities can perform very well, you are typically giving up some upside potential to eliminate downside market risk. So, it is a good idea to have some of your retirement money in investments that can capture more of the upside when the market is performing well. I guess the bottom line here is diversification.

By the way, when I speak of diversification, I am not referring to Bob, a client who was in my office a while back. I noticed he had small CDs at several different banks that all gave him about the same return. I asked him what his thinking was. His response? "Well, I've always heard I should diversify my investments." Somehow, he missed the fact that diversification means varying types of investments, not the same investment in a bunch of different banks.

A well-constructed, retirement-friendly portfolio will be diversified across asset classes. Some investments mitigate or eliminate downside market risk and produce guaranteed income, while others are less risk averse and liquid, taking full advantage of a booming market. Stay tuned for details!

As for the question at the beginning of this chapter, you'll have to make your own determination about FIAs making the list of the wonders of the world. But there's one thing that definitely needs to be added to the list — the deep-fried PB&J at the Oklahoma State Fair!

"If there is anyone to whom I owe money, I'm prepared to forget it if they are."

— Errol Flynn

"Wealth is worthless in the day of wrath, but righteousness delivers from death."

Proverbs 11:4

Chapter 6

The Fine Line Between Taking a Calculated Risk and Doing Something Stupid

Let's assume for a moment that you see the rationale in using FIAs as a means to help meet your nondiscretionary income needs (aka paycheck) in retirement, which makes you smarter than I look.

Great! You are on your way to swanning! So, let's move on to the fun part, options for your discretionary spending (aka play-check).

Dividend-Paying Large-Cap Stocks

While I wouldn't recommend putting a large percentage of your assets into individual stocks because of the risk that can be involved, they can be an option for a portion of your assets, depending upon your appetite for market volatility.

Why large cap? The term "large cap" means the company has a market capitalization in excess of $10 billion. These are typically well-established, but not necessarily profitable, companies.

Why dividend-paying? If a company is paying a dividend, it usually means the company is profitable. Companies with no profit can pay dividends, but it is not a common practice. So, what we are talking about here are big, (usually) profitable companies, which translates to less risk and volatility for you, the investor.

Here's a brief foray into how dividends work. Please forgive me if you already know this, or if you are an engineer and know everything, but allow me to offer the following example:

Let's say you own 100 shares of IBM. When they pay a dividend, they are, in essence, returning a portion of the company's profit to you, the owner. Wait, did I call you an owner of IBM? Yes, I did. Because that is what you are when you purchase their stock, an owner. Now, I will grant you that there may also be 100 million other owners, but still, you own a portion of the company.

As I write this, IBM's stock is at $138, and they pay an annual dividend of $6.48. So, for every share of IBM stock you own, they will return $6.48 in profit to you each year, which amounts to 4.7% (known as the dividend yield). But here's the great thing — regardless of whether the stock goes up or down in value, as long as the board of directors doesn't decide otherwise (which is highly unlikely in the case of IBM), you will get a dividend payment.

So, if you own 100 shares, IBM is going to pay you $648 each year in dividends. In a year in which the stock price doesn't change, or maybe even goes down, you still get your $648. But in years where the price of the stock goes up, you get the $648 PLUS the appreciation of the stock. Cool, right? I thought you'd agree.

Dennis came in to see me a while back after hearing my radio show. When I looked at his investments, I noticed he had several hundred thousand dollars in corporate and municipal bonds. As I mentioned in an earlier chapter, a bond is a loan. When you "buy" a bond, you are giving the company or government entity a loan. In return, they pay you a fixed rate of interest, which in Dennis' case, averaged about 3% yearly. When I inquired about his choice of investments, he explained that his soon-to-be ex-advisor had recommended bonds as a way to produce income.

Here is a paraphrase of the conversation that ensued:

Me:	Dennis, your advisor is correct, these bonds do produce income for you, but there is a problem.
Dennis:	Really? What's that?
Me:	You are 63 now. Do you think you could live another 30 years?
Dennis:	I don't see why not. Both of my parents lived into their 90s, and I am in excellent health.
Me:	That's great. Thirty years ago, a first-class postage stamp was 25 cents. As we speak, they are 55 cents. That is an increase of 120%.
Dennis:	I don't see where you're going with this. I haven't used stamps since Al Gore invented the internet.
Me:	This isn't about stamps; it's about the fact that the cost of living will rise dramatically over the next 30 years just as it has over the last 30 years.
Dennis:	So what?
Me:	How much will the $300,000 in bonds that you now own be worth in 30 years?
Dennis:	Um, $300,000?

Me:	Exactly. And how much income will those bonds be producing assuming the companies don't go bust?
Dennis:	I guess the same as it is now, about $9,000 per year.
Me:	Right. So, will $9,000 buy you the same number of stamps or amount of milk or bread or movie tickets in 30 years as it does today?
Dennis:	(after a long pause) Oh, I think I'm starting to get it. My $300,000 will still be $300,000, but it will not get me nearly as far.
Me:	Ding, ding, ding. Exactly. Bonds were a great idea for retirement portfolios a generation or two ago when we retired at 65 and died at 70, but today, not so much.
Dennis:	So, what should I do?
Me:	I thought you'd never ask. I would recommend, rather than being a creditor, you become an owner. You do this by buying a company's stock rather than loaning them money through bonds.
Dennis:	I'm listening.
Me:	Let me give you an extreme but very real example. If you had purchased $10,000 worth of Mastercard stock in 2006, that investment is now worth $612,772. Not bad. Even better, that original $10,000 is now paying you about $3,000 each year in dividends — a 30% return every year on your initial investment! If you had taken that same $10,000 and bought a 3% bond, it would still be worth $10,000 and still paying you a paltry $300/year.
Dennis:	I think I'm going to be sick.

Such is the beauty of high-quality, dividend-paying stocks, and they can be a great complement to your no-market-risk investments.

You may have gathered from my conversation with Dennis that I am not a fan of bonds. I am not saying I never recommend bonds, as there is a time and place for them, but, unlike many other advisors, I do not regularly use them as a place to park the "safe" part of your portfolio. Remember, we have already laid the foundation of your portfolio by generating lifetime income with FIAs. Why do we need a typically nonguaranteed, inferior alternative like bonds? We don't.

I do want to be sure you understand here that even though dividend-paying stocks can be a good idea for the less risk-averse investor, keep in mind that there are no guarantees with dividends. The company can stop the dividend payment at any point, and there is also the risk that the company could go broke.

Look at General Electric, for example. They were one of the darlings of the dividend-paying, blue-chip, large-cap stock world for decades. Now, not so much. Their dividend yield has gone from almost 12% in 2009 to 0.62% in July of 2020. But that's not even the worst part. The stock price has gone from around $30 as recently as late 2016 to $6.86 in July 2020. So before jumping into this type of investment, be certain you have the stomach (and the money) for the risk that can be involved.

Exchange-Traded Funds and Mutual Funds

Exchange-traded funds (ETFs) are a great way to provide diversification to your retirement portfolio without the fees that can be associated with mutual funds. ETFs are a basket of securities that trade much like individual stocks. They can be bought or sold anytime the market is open.

One such ETF that goes by the ticker symbol SPY is designed to track the S&P 500. SPY owns stocks such as Apple, Microsoft, Amazon, and Facebook, to name a few. So, the idea is that rather than buying these stocks individually, you can own all of them by buying one ETF. Other popular ETFs are DIA, which tracks the Dow Industrials; QQQ, which tracks the NASDAQ; and the IMW, which tracks the Russell 2000. And guess what? You can even buy ETFs that own dividend-paying stocks! It's the best of both worlds.

Clients often ask me to explain the difference between ETFs and mutual funds. They are similar in that they both own baskets of securities, but there are some essential differences.

❶ The first and foremost difference is a disparity in expenses that are charged to you, the shareholder.

For example, Mary originally came to our office to have her trust done by our estate planning team. Once the trust was executed, I invited Mary into my office to explain the process of funding her trust and the steps that she needed to take. We ultimately got into a discussion about her investment portfolio. Mary explained that she felt as if her investments were doing very well and did not see a reason to change anything. You know where this is going, don't you?

After she reluctantly agreed to allow me to give her a free second opinion, she changed her tune. Come to find out that, although her advisor's fee was a middle of the road 1.75%, she was paying another 1.5% in mutual fund fees, also known as an expense ratio. This meant that on her $500,000 portfolio over 10 years, she had generously "donated" $75,000 to the mutual fund companies for the privilege of owning their funds.

This situation is not unusual. While some mutual funds have reasonable ownership costs associated with them, many of them are in excess of 2.5%-3%. Ouch! Now, I am not saying that ETFs won't have any ownership expenses associated with them. But on average and with assistance from a decent advisor (call me, and I'll give you his name), you'll find that ETFs are less expensive to own.

> ❷ Yet another expense associated with mutual funds is called the "load."

Steve and Lois met with me recently because they were unhappy with their current advisor. Lois had recently rolled her 401(k) into an IRA, which the advisor promptly placed in front-loaded mutual funds. These are mutual funds that charge a fee or "load" to an investor when the fund is purchased. In Lois' case, the load was more than 5%. In other words, the $200,000 she invested instantly turned into $190,000, which meant that she had to have a gain of $10,000 to get back to even. Lois was not a happy camper. And to make matters worse, there really isn't a way to "undo" this once the investment is made. Lois had two choices, redeem the funds now and take a significant hit, or wait until her funds were over $200,000 again before doing any redemption. (The issue, of course, is that there is no way of knowing if the investment will EVER get back over $200,000.)

> ❸ Another difference between ETFs and mutual funds is the way they are taxed. Please keep in mind that I AM NOT A TAX GUY, so double-check with your tax professional to make sure I'm not misinformed or a downright dunderhead when it comes to this subject.

Remember, mutual funds are "baskets" of stocks. The stocks inside this basket are continually being bought and sold, thereby generating capital gains (if they are sold for a profit) for you, the investor. Depending on your income, these capital gains could be taxable in the year in which they are generated.

ETFs, on the other hand, are not taxable until you sell the entire ETF, thereby giving them a tax advantage over mutual funds.

However, this advantage goes away if the funds are inside an IRA — because IRA gains are not taxable, regardless of the investment, until the investments are sold at a profit. Make sense? If not, let me put it another way, when it comes to taxation, ETFs good, mutual funds, not so much.

To make ETF investments even more attractive, we collaborate with trading partners that use mathematical calculations to determine the most opportune times to enter and exit the market. Take a look at the chart below:

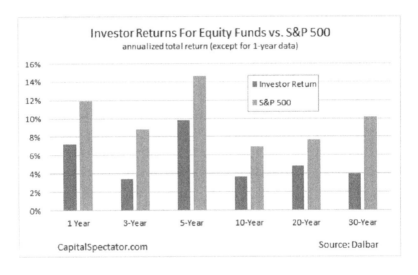

Source: CapitalSpectator.com

In this study by Dalbar, you can see that over the last 30 years, the typical do-it-yourself individual investor had an average return of 4%, while the S&P averaged over 10%. Rather than buying low and selling high, the individual investor tends to buy high and sell low. Why? Emotions! Years ago, Dr. James Dobson wrote a fascinating book entitled "Emotions: Can You Trust Them?" He used 166 pages to say, "NO!"

Here's what tends to happen. When the market is going gangbusters, investors get understandably excited and know without a doubt that the market will keep going up forever. Unfortunately, this exuberance reaches a fever pitch when the market nears a top, which means that many investors who have gotten their latest stock tips from their bookie are entering the market at the exact time they should be exiting.

On the other end of the spectrum, investors are the most discouraged, depressed, and downright hopeless when the market is nearing a bottom, and they tend to liquidate some or all of their positions, only to be met with the beginnings of a raging bull market. You've heard "buy low and sell high"? Well, without proper guidance, individual investors actually tend to buy high and sell low. Not a great strategy for wealth accumulation.

Perhaps one of the most egregious examples of emotional investing gone wrong occurred in 1976 when a guy by the name of Ronald Wayne sold his 10% stake in Apple for $800. Apparently, Wayne sold his stake as a result of a bad experience with a slot machine business he had previously owned, and he couldn't stand the thought of losing his Apple investment too — clearly an emotional decision, and not a very good one.

Any guesses as to what that 10% is worth today? Only around $100,000,000,000. That is $100 billion. So, if you ever think you're having a bad day, just remember Ronald Wayne.

To avoid a similar fate, the trading partners we work with take the emotions and guesswork out of investment decisions. They use mathematical, mechanical algorithms that closely track market and economic conditions to determine the optimal amount of market exposure for your investments at any given time. No guesswork, no emotions. In effect, you are maximizing upside while simultaneously minimizing (though not eliminating) your downside risk.

This process is known as dynamic rebalancing. Your investments are reallocated "on the fly," without so much as a phone call or email from you, if you're comfortable with that.

The way one of these trading partners puts it is that their strategy aims to capture 70%-80% of the market upside while avoiding 70%-80% of the downside. The result can be an exponential increase in investment returns when compared to manual rebalancing or buy and hold. While the S&P has returned around 500% over the last 20 years or so, using this strategy would have resulted in a 1,500% gain (300% better than buy and hold).

Again, keep in mind that we are not talking about guarantees here, and these strategies do involve the risk of loss. Nevertheless, this approach can be an invaluable method to eliminate the emotional mistakes commonly made by the average investor.

Some of the investments I do not typically recommend for retirement accounts due to excessive risk and volatility include:

- International funds or stocks
- Initial public offerings (IPOs)
- Small-cap stocks and funds
- Certain individual stocks or funds that are concentrated in pharmaceutical companies, energy companies, or emerging markets to name a few
- Penny stocks
- Commodities
- Futures
- Currencies
- Naked options (Yes, they're a real thing, and I know they sound like they could be fun, but you don't want them in a retirement account!)

Now, before you start mumbling about your neighbor's second cousin's wife's uncle who made a killing in penny stocks while he was on death row, let me remind you that I said I do not TYPICALLY RECOMMEND them. These types of investments are not always unwise or unprofitable. The question is, are they suitable or appropriate for your individual retirement portfolio? Typically, the answer to that question is no, but, of course, there are exceptions.

If you are like our federal government and have more money than you could ever spend, by all means, flush some of it down the crapper with penny stocks. This topic relates to risk tolerance, which we discussed earlier. But it's not just the risk that is involved with these types of investments; it is the volatility.

A few months ago, when the hysteria over the COVID-19 pandemic began, some energy companies lost 75% or more of their value in just a few days. *I know, I know, they always come back, that's just part of the boom and bust cycle of that market.* While that may be true in most instances, there are the occasional exceptions of companies that actually go broke. Remember when we discussed the concept of swanning? Well, sleeping well at night and volatility do not usually go together. On the other hand, if you like the excitement of potentially going from the penthouse to the poorhouse overnight, have at it.

Pharmaceutical companies often follow this pattern. News reports say the company is getting close to the elusive "diet pill" that promises a 30-pound weight loss in the first week while allowing you to fill up on pizza, ice cream, and cookies, and the stock goes through the roof overnight. A month later, when the clinical trials begin to show that one of the side effects is random hair growth on your teeth, the stock tanks.

These are but a few of the investments available to the less risk averse, but I will spare you the tedium of going through all of them. The general rule of thumb, which I alluded to earlier, is that there aren't good or bad investments, only suitable or unsuitable investments for your particular situation and appetite for risk — all of which we'll cover in detail when you and I get together!

"Money and women are the most sought after and the least known about of any two things we have."

— Will Rogers

"Keep your lives free from the love of money and be content with what you have, because God has said, 'Never will I leave you; never will I forsake you.'"

Hebrews 13:5

Chapter 7

And I Thought IRAs and 401(k)s Were a Good Thing

If you did not know, IRAs, 401(k)s, and 403(b)s and many other combinations of letter and numbers are known as pretax or qualified accounts. That means the money you put into them is tax-deferred. Notice I said tax-deferred, not tax-free.

The income tax on these accounts WILL have to be paid at some point. If not by you, then by your heirs, such as that good-for-nothing, Texas-Longhorn-supporting, semiprofessional surfer son-in-law or your beautiful, wonderful, perfect, adorable grandchildren. I like to call this your IRA becoming an IOU to the IRS!

So, while these qualified accounts are a great way to avoid paying income taxes in the short term, they can later become quite a burden. The idea is that you are deferring the income tax during your working years, while you are in a higher tax bracket, to your retirement years, when you are, at least in theory, in a lower tax bracket.

As you may already know, once you pass age 72, you will be required to gradually take money out of these accounts, known as required minimum distributions, or RMDs. Since no tax has yet been paid on these accounts, the RMD is fully taxable, thereby ensuring that our increasingly greedy, bloated, and dysfunctional government gets their tax money.

So why is this a problem? Let me give you an example:

Ronald and Patricia, who are in their early 60s, came to our office to have their trust drawn up by our estate attorney. While guiding them through the trust-funding process, I learned that they had about $10 million in their various investment accounts, nearly all of it qualified. Let me first say that I found it odd that their other advisor had not said anything to them about the importance of having a trust. Actually, it is not just odd; it's malpractice. You have $10 million with no plan in place to effectively distribute the funds after your demise, and no one has advised you otherwise? Really?

Anyway, their sole financial objective in life was to pass all their money onto their children. Yes, all $10 million. The plan was that they would live on just their Social Security and pension income, thereby maximizing their very generous gift to their kids.

We calculated that with a reasonable return on their investments, their $10 million could easily grow to $20 or $30 million by the time they were no longer counted in the census.

Here's where the problem comes in. Ronald and Patricia were oblivious to the fact that if their plan worked as designed, their children would be stuck with an enormous tax bill on the inheritance — not only income tax but inheritance tax on everything over $22,800,000. Inheritance tax is probably the most insidious tax of all. Couples can pass a total of $11,400,000 on to each other without being taxed, but if they attempt to pass a combined total of more than $22,800,000 on to heirs, they could end up paying 40% in federal inheritance taxes, plus state inheritance tax. This is nothing more than a money grab from our government. A way to "level the playing field" between the haves and the have-nots. Also known as redistribution of wealth, aka socialism.

OK, I'm off my soapbox. The bottom line with this couple is that the $20 or $30 million they believed would pass on to the kids would ultimately not end up being anywhere near that. Needless to say, they were shocked.

But, you say, I don't have anywhere near that much money, so I don't have to worry about it. Not so fast. While the inheritance tax only applies to those with estates over $22,800,000, income tax must be paid on the qualified account regardless of the amount. Even if you were planning on leaving your "paltry" $50,000 or $100,000 IRA to your kids, a substantial portion would magically go bye-bye after the government gets their income tax.

So how do we deal with this issue? Simple, we use something called, wait for it ... life insurance! Life insurance proceeds are completely tax-free for the beneficiaries. There are numerous ways to design a tax mitigation plan using life insurance, but let me continue with the example of Ronald and Patricia.

For this couple, we used something called a second-to-die life insurance policy, which pays out to the beneficiary only upon the death of the second insured. So, with Ronald and Patricia, the life insurance proceeds would pass to their kids after the second spouse becomes living challenged.

The great thing about using life insurance in this type of arrangement is the incredible leverage it can provide. Ronald and Patricia would pay a one-time premium of about $4.1 million in exchange for tax-free life insurance proceeds of about $14 million to the kids after the parents died. Leveraging $4.1 million that they don't really need for $14 million to their kids? Not a bad deal. Or to put it in terms the average investor might better understand, leveraging $41,000 and turning it into $140,000 — not too shabby. Just to be clear, in Ronald and Patricia's case, the estate and/or income taxes do not go away. Instead, the taxes are significantly mitigated by the $14 million in tax-free cash their children will receive. The kids will still have an obscenely high tax bill to deal with upon their parent's death, but now they have $14 million cash in hand to give Uncle Sam his unconscionable share. *Do you think Uncle Sam ever feels guilty? I don't think so either.*

This type of strategy is most effective when:

- You have qualified money that you are planning to pass on to someone other than your spouse
- You have an estate that is or will be valued over $11.4 million for individuals or $22.8 million for couples
- You have funds you can use to pay a life insurance premium that you or your spouse will not need for income
- You are in reasonably good health; remember, this is life insurance we're talking about, you'll need to qualify for it

Life insurance is the ultimate form of leverage. You can take a relatively small investment and leverage it into three or four times the original amount. *Pretty cool.*

Some of the other ways we use leverage (life insurance) in our retirement planning strategies:

> When you are in the unfortunate position of heading into retirement with a significant amount of debt

Life insurance can be an excellent method of making sure your spouse is not burdened by those debts in the event you go on a permanent vacation. Even if all we are talking about here is a mortgage, why leave your spouse with that debt when it can easily be taken care of with some decent life insurance planning?

> When you would like to leave a definite amount to your heirs

Ralph and Alice came into my office the other day after attending a retirement planning workshop I led at the University of Central Oklahoma. They made it very clear that leaving money to their kids was a priority. Naturally, my question to them was, "How much would you like to leave them?"

Both of them seemed a bit perplexed, and after a long silence, Alice blurted out, "Whatever is left."

Similar to the case study with Ronald and Patricia that I mentioned earlier, I went on to explain to Ralph and Alice that there is a way to leave a predetermined, guaranteed, tax-free amount to their kids by using the miracle of life insurance. *(OK, maybe I'm overstating it bit. After all, we are not talking about raising Lazarus.)*

This strategy also works very well if you would like to leave a predetermined amount to a worthy charity like the Marijuana Policy Project Foundation or the Clinton Foundation. *Your church might be a better option.* By making your charity the beneficiary on your life insurance policy, once again, you are leveraging a relatively small premium into a tax-free windfall for your charity. And who knows, maybe you'll even get a plaque with your name on it on one of the pews.

> When your spouse is going to come up short on income once you've left the building

We'll talk a bit more about this in the Social Security section, but if you are the primary breadwinner (or if there is a significant age disparity between you and your spouse), life insurance is a method of assuring that they will have adequate funds to sustain their lifestyle.

If you have lots of cash sitting around earning little or nothing, you do not like risks associated with the market, and you want that money to be liquid, then I have the perfect solution. This strategy uses something called an indexed universal life policy. This type of life insurance will allow you to leverage your money and get market-based returns with no downside market risk, and the funds remain liquid.

Kenny and Margaret stopped by my office the other day after being referred to me by an existing client. They needed some direction with their investments and asked me to put together a plan for them. Of course, I was happy to oblige. Among other things, Kenny had about $100,000 in cash that was sitting in a savings account and earning nearly .000000001%. So, I did an illustration for him using the previously mentioned indexed universal life policy.

Here's what it showed:

- His $100,000 would instantly turn into a $163,000 tax-free benefit to Margaret when he kicks the oxygen habit. (It earned an average of 7.95% over the last 20 years. This is not a guarantee going forward, of course, just an example of what is possible. Keep in mind that although the return will fluctuate, it cannot be less than zero.)

- It would provide a benefit of $122,750 if Kenny were diagnosed with a terminal illness.

- And the icing on the cake ...
- The $100,000 investment was liquid! He could surrender the policy at any time and not get back less than his original investment.

One more thing: Underwriting requirements are relaxed on this type of product. Since you are making an up-front investment, the insurance company is not as concerned with your health history as it would be with a traditional life insurance policy.

So, if you have a large sum of what we call "lazy money" sitting around (cash, CDs, money market accounts, etc.), this could be just the ticket.

To summarize, life insurance ain't what it used to be. The days of the old, overpriced, underperforming whole-life policy have been replaced by some well-designed, practical, and innovative products that can fill a variety of needs.

"People are living longer than ever before, a phenomenon undoubtedly made necessary by the 30-year mortgage."

— Doug Larson

"Do not wear yourself out to get rich; do not trust your own cleverness."

Proverbs 23:4

Chapter 8

Do I Need Professional Help?

A while back, I came across this "The Far Side" cartoon:

Don't worry; we are not talking about THAT kind of professional help but the type of professional help that you may need when planning for retirement or managing your existing retirement portfolio.

Following are but a few of the many situations that could call for this type of "therapy":

There is a significant age gap between you and your spouse

Age differences can be a tricky situation for some married couples. Recently, one of my clients, Steve, showed up to my office without his wife. As I usually do during the "Where are you?" process, I asked him about his current Social Security benefits. His were around $3,000/month, and his wife's were about $2,000/month. I then asked him if he knew what happens to their Social Security benefits when one of them passes away. He responded that no, he did not know and hadn't really thought about it.

When I explained to him that the surviving spouse would only receive the higher of the two benefits, he was quite surprised and very concerned. The problem here, as is often the case, is that he was around 15 years older than his wife, which means that if he passed away first, which was very likely, his wife would start receiving his $3,000/month benefit, but she would lose hers, a drop in their household income of $2,000/month. *Not a problem if he were like our government and could just print money willy-nilly.*

In their case, however, it was taking pretty much all their $5,000/month Social Security income to make ends meet, so a loss of $2,000/month would be devastating for his widow. But never fear, your trusty retirement planning professional had an answer!

In this case, I advised him to take a portion of his retirement funds and set them up to generate guaranteed lifetime income for himself AND his wife. This strategy more than compensates for the loss of Social Security income when Steve assumes room temperature. And since it was guaranteed, there is no concern of it ever running out no matter how long his wife lives.

In essence, what we did is use some of his retirement savings to create a lifetime pension, something he did not have from his employer. The crazy thing here, though, is that his current "advisor" never had this conversation with him, which, of course, is why "advisor" is in quotes. How can you call yourself an advisor if you have not had the most basic of discussions with your clients regarding things like the financial ramifications of a spouse dying? Which is a beautiful segue into the next reason you may need professional help:

You've recently lost a spouse who handled most of the investment decisions

Widows are some of the more frequent callers on my radio show. Often, their husbands handled most or all of the decisions regarding their investments, and once they're gone, the widows are absolutely lost. These women are not only mourning (maybe) the loss of their husbands, but they are also overwhelmed with making financial decisions that they're not equipped to make.

It is a very sad situation, but one that can usually be remedied with the help of a professional (like me).

When I do retirement planning for couples, I try, to the degree it's possible, to design plans that are seamless when one spouse dies. In other words, the surviving spouse has to make very few, if any, major decisions regarding their retirement plan. In so doing, I am significantly reducing the odds of the surviving spouse becoming one of the previously mentioned callers to my radio show.

Let me add here that, on occasion, I will have one spouse come into my office without the other spouse. While there can certainly be legitimate reasons, it is critically important that whenever possible, I meet with both husband and wife. Think about it. If you are married, and you are the primary breadwinner and investment guru, isn't it just as important, if not more so, for your spouse to meet with me as it is for you to meet with me?

Keep in mind that there may come a time when your spouse (usually the lovely bride) will need to handle things without you. It would be an excellent idea — not to mention a loving gesture — for her or him to be brought up to speed on what the heck is going on with your finances and investments.

You do not have a trust

Seriously? Does this actually happen? Unfortunately, YES! Again, no retirement/financial plan is complete without at least a discussion of the potential need for a trust. But I'd say probably around 50% of the people who walk into our offices find themselves in such a situation.

The most extreme example I have seen is probably Barry and Patricia's situation. Their retirement savings totaled somewhere around $15 million, and their "advisor" never had a conversation with them about the importance of having a trust. Crazy.

I also have folks with trusts come in, but their advisor or trust attorney has never explained to them that for a trust to do what it is designed to do, the assets need to be placed in the trust. We call this process "trust funding" and guide you through this step as part of our estate planning services.

So, if you have a trust, and it hasn't been funded, you don't actually have a trust; you have a mostly worthless document that may do little or nothing for your heirs.

You don't know specifically how your portfolio has performed historically, what the fees are, what you are invested in, or your specific investment strategy

When Stan and Hannah were in my office, I asked about their investment strategy. They responded with, "Here, take our money."

They were being facetious to some degree, but the point was that they knew very little about their current investments, which, to say the least, is quite troublesome. For all they knew, everything they had was invested in Woolworth stock, and they are risk-averse retirees. As I've said at least 100 times so far, retirement is no time to find yourself in a situation where you are vulnerable to huge losses. So, if you can't tell me what your approximate return has been for the last few years, along with what your advisor's fee is, your investment mix, or even your advisor's name, we need to talk. And if you can't tell me YOUR name, we have an entirely different issue on our hands.

You have your investments scattered among many different accounts/advisors

This situation can be quite problematic. The challenge here is that it makes it very tough, if not impossible, to have a cohesive strategy of any kind. It's like trying to herd cats; everything is going in different directions. Your investments need to function as players on a team, all with the same objective.

Also, the more scattered your investments, the more complicated, time consuming, and downright confusing it can be to keep track of things.

You are depending on your retirement savings for income

This situation is not one to take lightly. If you NEED income from your investments, you simply cannot afford to make mistakes with your planning, which calls for careful strategizing from a qualified professional. I think I may know just the guy.

You own a variable annuity

We discussed these mostly crappy products in a previous chapter, so I will not go on ad nauseam about this. But if you thought your retirement funds were safe because you own a VA, think again! As we discussed earlier, these annuities are exposed to stock market risk, usually have very high fees, and may or may not provide lifetime income.

If you own a VA or think you may own one, call me — STAT! When you come in, we will call the company that underwrote your VA together and find out directly from the horse's mouth what the fees and various risks are to your particular VA.

You've left a 401(k) with a previous employer

Why in the world would someone retire, get canned, or otherwise tell their employer to take this job and shove it and not take their 401(k) with them? Most often, it's because they don't know any better. Sandra came in to see me and brought her various account statements with her. Among the documents were statements from four different 401(k)s, all from former employers. In talking with her, I found out that she thought those accounts had to remain where they were until she was fully retired. As you may have guessed, I set her straight.

When you leave an employer, you have every right to move that 401(k) to your new 401(k) if you have one, or better yet, roll it into an IRA, all without income tax liability. There are several reasons to consider this. First of all, it's easy to ignore or forget about old accounts. Your retirement accounts need ATTENTION regularly, hopefully from a professional, much like me, for them to perform according to your goals and objectives.

Another reason to move your old 401(k)s into IRAs, is to simplify your life, and whose life doesn't need simplifying? Sandra was quite relieved to know that she could consolidate all her old 401(k)s into one IRA that she could keep track of with just a couple clicks of a mouse.

Another thing on this subject: Most 401(k)s do not offer you the vast array of investment options that are available to you through an independent investment advisor. While you may be able to choose from various life-cycle or mutual funds, some of the more sophisticated and often more desirable investments will be out of reach with your 401(k). You may also be limited to the frequency with which you may rebalance your accounts. Some 401(k)s that I've seen will only allow you to change your investment mix every quarter, which could spell disaster in a volatile market.

Perhaps the most important reason to take your 401(k) with you when you leave your employer is that if the company should happen to be sold or go out of business, your 401(k) money could be tied up until the Thunder win the NBA championship. This is especially concerning with the current state of affairs in the financial markets. Companies are being bought, sold, and going belly up at an alarming rate, which makes leaving your 401(k) behind a truly risky and totally unnecessary proposition.

> Bottom line: When you leave your employer, take your 401(k) with you!

There are almost as many of these situations that present themselves as there are clients. But if any of these ring true for you, let's get you into therapy. I promise not to label you as Just Plain Nuts. On second thought, I probably shouldn't guarantee that before we even meet!

> "Too many people spend money they haven't earned, to buy things they don't want, to impress people they don't like."
>
> — Will Smith

"Better a little with the fear of the Lord than great wealth with turmoil."

Proverbs 15:6

Chapter 9

Is It Time to Defund?

No, I'm not talking about the police. Are you crazy? Do you really think I would even attempt to address that in this forum? Jeez. Give me some credit here. I'm asking about defunding (aka firing) your current advisor — an age-old question that is right up there with: Who closes the bus door when the driver gets off? Who put the alphabet in alphabetical order? What exactly is the purpose of the pinky toe? And what are the odds that Lou Gehrig would end up with Lou Gehrig's disease?

OK, OK, so maybe it isn't quite in the same category as those questions, but it certainly is a critical issue. So, here are some of the reasons firing your advisor (and hiring me) might be worth considering:

The Demographics Don't Fit

What in the world do demographics have to do with anything? Well, if you have had the (mostly) wonderful experience of having children, you may know where I am going with this. There is this thing called PERSPECTIVE that can be all important when it comes to designing your retirement plan. Between the ages of

12 and 25 or so, kids are pretty much knuckleheads, which, unfortunately, sometimes never goes away. But usually around their mid-20s, kids start to get a clue. My wife and I call it "coming out of the tunnel." One of the reasons for the epiphanies they seem to have is that their perspective on life begins to change. They realize their parents aren't the fools they once thought them to be — maybe the swastika tattoo on their forehead wasn't such a great idea — and that sometimes unanswered prayers can be a great blessing!

Here is where demographics come in. Let's say you have an advisor who is much younger than you (and me) are. They are likely thinner and more attractive than I am, but their youthfulness could be an issue. They may be very well versed in the financial markets, but their perspective could be skewed. While they may not have an obscene tattoo on their forehead, it can be difficult for them to relate to the concerns of a retiree or near retiree. Have they seen firsthand the devastation of a severe market meltdown? Do they know the anxiety that can come with worrying about running out of money? Do they understand the frustration that comes from constantly misplacing your reading glasses or having to pee every 10 minutes? OK, that one really isn't relevant, but I think you get the idea. Younger advisors tend to use riskier investment strategies and may not take the precautions necessary to protect your retirement funds for the long term.

Granted, that is a broad generalization. Obviously, not all younger advisors fall into this category. Come to think of it; I was young once. But it just might be something for you to consider when choosing the person who will advise you on some of the most important financial decisions you'll ever make.

Another demographic issue has to do with the average age and/or socioeconomic status of a particular advisor's clients. Does your advisor specialize in working with clients within your age range and economic background? Or do they attempt to be general practitioners and not really specialize in anything at all? Advisors simply cannot effectively be all things to all people, although many of them attempt to be, and this can be an issue. If you knew you had a serious heart issue, for instance, would you continue going to your internal medicine doctor to treat it, or would you maybe go to a cardiologist? Or, if you had a brain tumor, I certainly hope you would be seeing a neurologist and not your family medicine doctor.

Well, entering into your retirement years is akin to a serious medical issue in my book. The advice and counsel you receive is of critical importance and should be dispensed by a specialist as opposed to a general practitioner. As I have mentioned previously, our firm specializes in retirement planning. We do not attempt to be all things to all people.

Your Advisor Is Not a Fiduciary

As a fiduciary, I am legally and ethically obligated to act in my client's best interest. In my business, this typically requires a specific type of securities license.

Sonja's father heard my radio show and referred her to me. She was in a real pickle, so she came in to see me last week. Her 401(k) was with an employer that had recently laid her off, and she was having difficulty finding other employment. She wanted to set up an IRA into which she could transfer her 401(k), which I would normally be more than happy to do. You'll remember that in an earlier chapter, I told you that moving your 401(k) money from previous employers into an IRA is a must. Well, this was an exception!

The problem stemmed from Sonja being in between jobs. She was not in a position to have these funds actively managed or even invested; she may need to access them to help her through her period of unemployment. If she moved those funds to an

IRA, she would have to pay a monthly fee, albeit a small one, even if those funds were just in cash. Clearly, it would have been in MY best interest to help her set up the IRA. But it was in HER best interest to leave the funds in cash inside her 401(k) and not be subject to any fees, which is, of course, what I advised her to do. Now, I am certainly not saying that a nonfiduciary advisor would have counseled her any differently. Just because an advisor is not a fiduciary, it does not mean they WON'T act in your best interest.

What I'm saying is that if I take my fiduciary responsibility seriously, and I do, it brings clarity to my recommendations since acting in your best interest is my primary consideration.

Your Advisor Is an Employee of a Firm They Do Not Own

Have you ever gone to a Ford dealer and had them extol the virtues of a Chevy? Highly unlikely. Why? Because the person you talk to is an employee of the Ford dealership. As such, they are obligated to sell you Fords — lest they end up running the Tilt-A-Whirl at Six Flags.

Well, in my industry, there are what I refer to as independent advisors and captive advisors. As an independent advisor, I am self-employed and not beholden to any particular company's or organization's products — which allows me to offer my clients the (actual) best options for them. In contrast, a captive advisor is an employee of an investment company and is limited to offering clients only their employer's investment options, much as the Ford salesperson is limited to selling Fords.

While I may put together a plan for you using ETFs with very low, if any fees, the captive advisor may be obligated by his employer to put you into a costly mutual fund or, God forbid, a variable annuity. I run across these scenarios quite often.

For instance, when I met with Sue, she showed me her account statements from her current advisor, an employee of a particular investment company whose name you would surely recognize. Noticing that she had zero investments that had any guarantees of any kind, I explained to her that I really believed, given her financial situation and objectives, that it was essential for her to consider building her retirement portfolio on a foundation of guarantees. Her response? "Well, I would love to, but my current (soon-to-be former) advisor doesn't have any options for that."

The translation: My advisor is only permitted to offer what his employer tells him he can offer, and safety is not an option.

How can you tell which category a particular advisor falls into? Easy, ASK! You might pose the following questions:

- Are you an employee of a particular company, or are you completely independent?
- Are you limited by the company you work for as to the investment options you can offer?
- Do you have the universe of investment options at your disposal?

Your advisor has not made any substantive changes to your investments, or at least discussed this with you, as you entered into your retirement years

My wife and I have five wonderful daughters. We had numerous vehicles when they were young — ranging from Suburbans to an obnoxious high-top Ford conversion van. But our favorite was the Chevy 12-passenger van. You may be asking why we needed a 12-passenger van when there were only five kids. The answer is quite simple; so they wouldn't touch! If you have ever been fortunate enough to have driven long distances with multiple children (or even adults), you understand the importance of keeping them from touching.

Fast-forward a few years. Now I drive a sedan, and my wife drives a small SUV. So why the drastic change in vehicle choices? Simple. Our NEEDS changed, which is the same reason people often downsize their homes when the kids fly the coop. Well, our financial needs, objectives, and risk tolerance also change as we become "unyoung" — a fact that many advisors and their clients seem to overlook.

Often, people who come to my office tell me they have been with the same advisor for 10 or 20 years or more. In those cases, my first question is always, "When was the last time your investments were rebalanced — or at the very least reviewed to see if rebalancing is necessary?"

To my dismay, the answer to that question is often: I don't know, never, or I believe it was the year Oklahoma became a state (1907). Why is this important? Well, during your working years, your investments should be balanced toward growth. Safety is not generally a top priority. When you are closing in on retirement or already there, preservation becomes a more serious consideration. It does not mean we aren't interested in growth. Indeed, we are concerned with how your portfolio grows, but not at the expense of safety or preservation.

Of course, there are exceptions. If you have more money than you could ever spend, preservation may not be an issue. Unfortunately, most of us are not in this position. So, if you are, say, 70 years old, and your financial plan is much the same as it was when you were 50, you were likely too conservative with your investments when you were younger, or you're too aggressive now. Either way, you may not have received sound advice from your advisor. (Or you received sound advice but promptly ignored it.)

Here is a synopsis of a conversation I recently had with future clients Tim and Amanda:

Me:	What would you say are your top priorities for your retirement funds?
Clients:	Well, we need money to live on, of course, and we would like to leave something to the kids and our church.
Me:	That sounds good. So how have you structured your retirement plan to accomplish those goals?
Clients:	Huh?
Me:	Well, are your investments in line with what it is you want to accomplish?
Clients:	I guess so.
Me:	So what we are talking about here is capital preservation, right? If you need this money to live on, and you want to be sure you have something left for the kids and your church, these funds need to be allocated in such a way as to significantly mitigate the risks of a significant market downturn since you cannot leave money behind that doesn't exist. Would you agree?
Clients:	Definitely. That's why we are invested so conservatively.
Me:	What makes you think you are invested conservatively?
Clients:	That's what our advisor told us.
Me:	When did he tell you that?
Clients:	I believe it was around the time Neil Armstrong landed on the moon.
Me:	And when was the last time your portfolio was rebalanced to be sure it's still in alignment with your objectives?
Clients:	Like I said, when Neil Armstrong landed on the moon.
Me:	So, it hasn't been rebalanced since then?
Clients:	Umm. I guess not.

To make a short story long, Tim and Amanda had a large percentage of their funds in individual oil stocks and international mutual funds, investments that are about as conservative as Bernie Sanders. While these may have been somewhat appropriate for them when they were young, they certainly were not suitable now. Their ding-dong advisor had just not taken the time or did not care enough to make any adjustments along the way. Tim and Amanda fired him that very day!

Another issue here is that some of the investment strategies that were effective in the past may not be so great now. Have you ever heard of the buy and hold strategy? It simply refers to buying a particular stock and holding onto it forever. This strategy worked quite well for a long time. Now, not so much.

Here are the stocks that comprised the Dow Industrials in 1991:

- Allied Signal, Inc.
- Aluminum Company of America
- American Express
- AT&T
- Bethlehem Steel
- Boeing
- Caterpillar
- Chevron
- Coca-Cola
- DuPont
- Eastman Kodak
- Exxon
- General Electric

- General Motors
- Goodyear
- IBM
- International Paper
- J.P. Morgan
- McDonald's
- Merck
- 3M
- Philip Morris
- Proctor and Gamble
- Sears
- Texaco
- Union Carbide
- United Technologies
- Walt Disney
- Westinghouse
- Woolworth

As you may have noticed, many of these companies don't exist any longer. If you had invested $10,000 in each of these companies and intended to hold onto them forever — you would have lost, approximately, a lot of money on many of those investments.

I'm not saying that buying individual stocks and holding them for long periods is always a bad idea. It's just that this is a strategy that needs to be monitored closely and adjusted as needed. Scrutiny like that usually leads to adding stocks and kicking others to the curb. So, if your advisor is asleep at the wheel and has not made regular adjustments to your portfolio as you've aged, and the viability of some of the stocks you own has deteriorated, it may be time to kick your advisor to the curb, along with your Sears stock.

Your Advisor Is Constantly Making Changes to Your Portfolio

Yes, I know I just got finished saying that your investments need to be closely monitored and adjusted. However, there is a flip side. It is also possible that your positions are adjusted too often. If you are finding that your portfolio holdings are erratic and continually changing, it can be a sign that your advisor is commissioned based or has a severe case of attention deficit disorder. The problem with commission-only advisors is that they may get paid when they move you from one investment to another, which can sometimes lead to frequent and unnecessary alterations to your portfolio. In the financial industry, this is referred to as churning, and it is a big no-no. Unfortunately, it happens anyway.

So, if you are always getting trade confirmations via mail or email, you may want to take a closer look to be sure your advisor isn't churning your investments to line their pockets.

Following is a document from a well-known advisory firm, explaining to their potential advisors how they are compensated:

> **We earn our revenue primarily from our clients.**

> **We also earn revenue from product providers and money managers ('third parties') who assist us in providing the investments and services that we offer you.**

Our revenue from clients includes:

- Commissions you pay when you buy or sell equities and fixed-income investments (this applies when we act as agent or broker)

- Markups and markdowns on your price when you buy or sell securities (this applies when we act as principal outside of investment advisory programs, buying and selling from our own inventory, primarily for bonds)

- Sales loads (sales charges), commissions or concessions derived from the offering and sale of various managed investments such as mutual funds, unit investment trusts, insurance and annuities

- Transaction fees on the purchase or sale of certain equity and fixed-income products in brokerage accounts

- Fees based on the value of your assets in our advisory programs

- Interest on margin accounts

- Miscellaneous fees, including fees for IRAs, wire transfers, returned checks, transfer on death services, and money market fund low balances

Wow! Quite a list, isn't it? Do you think such an advisor might be inclined to move you into and out of different investments unnecessarily? By the way, advisors hired by this firm are employees. They are not independent, as we discussed earlier, and they have much less latitude with regards to investment options.

Incidentally, did you notice the part about "We also earn our revenue from product providers and money managers …"? The translation here is that this advisory firm may be inclined to push products that may or may not be appropriate for you because these third parties incentivize them to do so.

Your Advisor Does Not Engage in Comprehensive Retirement Planning

There is much more to retirement planning than investments. I often see clients whose "advisors" have not done much of anything other than investment management, leaving gaping holes in their retirement plan. If your advisor has not at least talked to you about the following, they are not a comprehensive retirement planner:

- Estate planning
- Life insurance planning
- Social Security planning
- Legacy planning
- Income planning
- Tax planning
- Long-term-care planning

Now I did not say that they necessarily need to DO all this planning. But, at the very least, your planner should have discussed these issues with you, given you direction, and referred you to a specialist if necessary.

At our firm, we tackle many of these planning needs in-house, making it much more convenient and consistent for our clients.

Finally, you may want to fire your advisor if ... they don't like Chick-fil-A. Just kidding (sort of).

If you're considering making an advisory and/or strategy change, ask your advisor the following questions (the answers to which should give you some insight into their motivation):

- How do you get paid?
- Are you paid a commission when you buy and sell my investments?
- Are you a fiduciary?
- How often do you review my investments?
- Are you limited in any way as to the investment options you can offer?
- Are you an employee of (company name)?
- What types of guaranteed options do you recommend (if any)? Why or why not?
- What is your specialty?
- What, if anything, makes you any different than any other advisor?
- Who is your favorite politician?
- How long have you been licensed?
- What professional credentials do you have?
- What kinds of returns have your recommendations been getting?

And, of course ...

- Who is your favorite Big 12 football team? (If the answer is anything other than OU or OSU ... run!)

"I don't understand people who say, 'I don't know how to thank you.' They never heard of money?"

— Anonymous

"But seek first the kingdom of God and his righteousness, and all these things will be added to you."

Matthew 6:33

Chapter 10

Don't Worry, Be Happy

Often, when I speak to a new or prospective client, they will have some level of apprehension about moving their investments for any number of reasons. As it turns out, many of the things clients are concerned about turn out to be relatively insignificant or nonissues at all once they completely understand the process.

In this chapter, I am going to address some of the more common concerns and questions I come across and examine how they may or may not affect us working together.

If I move my 401(k) from my current employer, won't I lose out on the company match?

In a word, no! We are not CLOSING your 401(k) account. We are merely moving what is in the 401(k) to a self-managed IRA. Imagine a bucket under a faucet. The bucket is your current 401(k), and what comes out of the faucet represents the deposits into your 401(k). All we are doing is taking the contents of that bucket, dumping it into a different bucket (your new IRA), and promptly placing the bucket back under the faucet so that your 401(k) continues just as it has.

Will I be taxed when I move my 401(k)?

You are taxed on your 401(k) when you actually take the funds out of the account and spend them on your new boat, new house, or burial plot for your cat. We are not spending anything. We are rolling your 401(k) into an IRA, also known as a ... wait for it ... rollover. When done correctly, rollovers are a nontaxable event.

What do I need to do to get my funds moved so you can manage them?

Sometimes, people are concerned about this because they would rather not talk to their former advisor. Or perhaps they are just wondering what the exact process is. Well, most of the time, all you need to do to facilitate opening an account with me is — sign a bunch of crap. That's it. Just signatures. There is usually no need to talk to your ex-advisor, as all we do is send their firm a transfer document.

I say "usually" because there is the occasional snafu, which, to resolve, may require some action on your part. Even then, we are typically dealing with the advisor's custodian (the firm that holds the funds, i.e., TD Ameritrade or Charles Schwab) and not the advisor directly.

How long does the process take?

That is an excellent question, and one I do not have an easy answer for. Typically, it takes between four to six weeks before everything is said and done, but it could be longer. Much of the timing depends on how quickly your current custodian completes their part of the transfer process. The problem here is that your former custodian is in no hurry to have your funds transferred. I know, shocking, right? When this happens, we, as your new advisors, may need to jump through any number of hoops to get things done. But we are well equipped to deal with these issues, as they occur fairly regularly.

Won't my old advisor be mad at me?

If they are worth their salt, yes! I typically ask my clients who are concerned about hurting their ex-advisors' feelings if that advisor would be willing to write them a check for any losses they may incur under his management. The answer, of course, is NO! Or, to put it another way, how much is it worth to you to spare your advisor's feelings? $10,000? $50,000? $100,000? It is purely a business decision; there's nothing personal about it.

Would you continue going to a doctor who you felt was giving you inferior advice even though you've known him since second grade? What if he were your golfing buddy; would that change your mind? What if you went to church together? What if you had shared a cell at Leavenworth? We are talking about your health here, so I would hope the answers to those questions would be a resounding NO!

Well, retirement investments are part of your financial health. While these may not be life-threatening decisions, they can certainly threaten your QUALITY of life. And if your advisor's planning (or lack thereof) causes you fear and/or anxiety, it could be life threatening.

Here's the thing, moving your accounts from your former, inferior advisor to our firm could be quite simple or slightly complex. Fortunately, for you, it doesn't make a difference. We are well prepared to handle all of the details for you so you can SWAN!

"Sometimes I just want someone to hug me and say, 'I know it's hard, but you'll be OK. Here's a coffee and a million dollars.'"

— Anonymous

"God's blessing makes life rich; nothing we do can improve on God."

Proverbs 10:22

Chapter 11

How to Maximize Your Social Security in One Easy Step

Live a really long time. The end.

In some ways, it is that simple. I have a software program that will produce a 28-page Social Security report that shows all the different claiming strategies to maximize your benefits.

But the degree to which those strategies are or are not effective is based on life expectancy, something most of us have very little control over. However, having a working knowledge of basic concepts is essential for everyone.

If you haven't already done so, go to SSA.gov and create an account for yourself and your spouse if you're hitched. For a government website, it is actually quite helpful and easy to navigate (which makes me think it was built by Bob's Websites, LLC, or some other nongovernmental entity). Once you create your account, you'll be able to view an up-to-date Social Security statement that looks like this:

Your Estimated Benefits

*Retirement You have earned enough credits to qualify for benefits. At your current earnings rate, if you continue working until...
your full retirement age (67 years), your payment would be about .... $ 1,743 a month
age 70, your payment would be about .... $ 2,222 a month
age 62, your payment would be about .... $ 1,143 a month

*Disability You have earned enough credits to qualify for benefits. If you became disabled right now your payment would be about .... $ 1,590 a month

*Family If you get retirement or disability benefits, your spouse and children also may qualify for benefits.

*Survivors You have earned enough credits for your family to receive survivors benefits. If you die this year, certain members of your family may qualify for the following benefits:
Your child .... $ 1,222 a month
Your spouse who is caring for your child .... $ 1,222 a month
Your spouse, if benefits start at full retirement age .... $ 1,629 a month
Total family benefits cannot be more than .... $ 2,936 a month
Your spouse or minor child may be eligible for a special one-time death benefit of $255.

Medicare You have enough credits to qualify for Medicare at age 65. Even if you do not retire at age 65, be sure to contact Social Security three months before your 65th birthday to enroll in Medicare.

* Your estimated benefits are based on current law. Congress has made changes to the law in the past and can do so at any time. The law governing benefit amounts may change because, by 2035, the payroll taxes collected will be enough to pay only about 80 percent of scheduled benefits.

We based your benefit estimates on these facts:
Your date of birth (please verify your name on page 1 and this date of birth) .... July 16, 1966
Your estimated taxable earnings per year after 2020 .... $44,350
Your Social Security number (only the last four digits are shown to help prevent identity theft) XXX-XX-2074

How Your Benefits Are Estimated

To qualify for benefits, you earn "credits" through your work — up to four each year. This year, for example, you earn one credit for each $1,410 of wages or self-employment income. When you've earned $5,640, you've earned your four credits for the year. Most people need 40 credits, earned over their working lifetime, to receive retirement benefits. For disability and survivors benefits, young people need fewer credits to be eligible.

We checked your records to see whether you have earned enough credits to qualify for benefits. If you haven't earned enough yet to qualify for any type of benefit, we can't give you a benefit estimate now. If you continue to work, we'll give you an estimate when you do qualify.

What we assumed — If you have enough work credits, we estimated your benefit amounts using your average earnings over your working lifetime. For 2020 and later (up to retirement age), we assumed you'll continue to work and make about the same as you did in 2018 or 2019. We also included credits we assumed you earned last year and this year.

Generally, the older you are and the closer you are to retirement, the more accurate the retirement estimates will be because they are based on a longer work history with fewer uncertainties such as earnings fluctuations and future law changes. We encourage you to use our online Retirement Estimator to obtain immediate and personalized benefit estimates.

We can't provide your actual benefit amount until you apply for benefits. **And that amount may differ from the estimates above because:**
(1) Your earnings may increase or decrease in the future.
(2) After you start receiving benefits, they will be adjusted for cost-of-living increases.

(3) Your estimated benefits are based on current law. **The law governing benefit amounts may change.**
(4) Your benefit amount may be affected by **military service, railroad employment or pensions earned through work on which you did not pay Social Security tax.** Visit *www.socialsecurity.gov* to learn more.

Windfall Elimination Provision (WEP) — If you receive a pension from employment in which you did not pay Social Security taxes and you also qualify for your own Social Security retirement or disability benefit, your Social Security benefit may be reduced, but not eliminated, by WEP. The amount of the reduction, if any, depends on your earnings and number of years in jobs in which you paid Social Security taxes, and the year you are age 62 or become disabled. To estimate WEP's effect on your Social Security benefit, visit *www.socialsecurity.gov/WEP-CHART*. For workers newly eligible in 2020, the maximum monthly reduction in PIA is $480. For more information, please see *Windfall Elimination Provision* (Publication No. 05-10045) at *www.socialsecurity.gov/WEP*.

Government Pension Offset (GPO) — If you receive a pension based on federal, state or local government work in which you did not pay Social Security taxes and you qualify, now or in the future, for Social Security benefits as a current or former spouse, widow or widower, you are likely to be affected by GPO. If GPO applies, your Social Security benefit will be reduced by an amount equal to two-thirds of your government pension, and could be reduced to zero. Even if your benefit is reduced to zero, you will be eligible for Medicare at age 65 on your spouse's record. To learn more, please see *Government Pension Offset* (Publication No. 05-10007) at *www.socialsecurity.gov/GPO*.

Source: SSA.gov

As you can see, this statement will tell you exactly what your benefits will be at various ages and circumstances. At the top, you'll see your full retirement age (FRA) and what your benefit would be if you started collecting it at that time. You will also see your benefit at age 62 and 70. In general, you can begin benefits as early as age 62, at which point you would receive approximately 70% of your benefits at your FRA. After your FRA, benefits increase at 8% per year until age 70.

Considerations for Collecting Earlier Versus Later

Life Expectancy

Your Lifetime Social Security Income Depends on When You Start and How Long You Live

Start Social Security at:	62 (earliest)	66 (FRA)	70 (latest)
Initial annual income:	$18,000	$24,240	$32,520
Live to 70, total lifetime income:	$144,000	$96,960	$0
Live to 80, total lifetime income:	$324,000	$339,360	$325,200
Live to 90, total lifetime income:	$504,000	$581,760	$650,400
	Best strategy if you die at 70	*Best strategy if you die at 80*	*Best strategy if you die at 90*

Source: CBS News

This chart shows the trade-offs associated with collecting earlier instead of later. As I already noted, life expectancy is a huge consideration when it comes to making this decision. Not surprisingly, as the chart shows, the longer you expect to live, the better off you are waiting to collect your benefits if you can. If you are in poor health or your ancestors were not blessed with longevity, you may want to consider taking your benefits earlier rather than later.

Financial Need

Even if you expect to live longer than Methuselah — who was 969 years old when he finally cashed it in — delaying your benefits may not be a great idea. It may not even be possible if you need your Social Security benefits to put food on the table or buy your grande iced sugar-free vanilla latte with soy milk every morning.

The Effect on Your Spouse's Benefits

If you are married, you will receive the greater of your benefit (or up to 50% of your spouse's). The spousal benefit is based on your spouse's benefit at their FRA. If your spouse delays their benefit beyond their FRA, it will not increase your spousal benefit. When I reread those last two sentences, it sounded ridiculously confusing. So, let's look at an example, which may also be confusing:

If Bob's benefit at his FRA is $2,000, and his wife, Carolyn's, benefit would be, say, $500, obviously it would be more advantageous for Carolyn to collect half of Bob's benefit ($1,000), than 100% of her own benefit. However, if Bob waits until 70 to collect, when his benefit would be $2,720, Carolyn's spousal benefit would still be stuck at half of Bob's FRA benefit, $1,000.

But the real issue here is that if Bob were to start collecting at age 62, when his benefit would be $1,500, the most Carolyn would ever receive as long as Bob is living is $750. In a nutshell, we've gone from a total household benefit of $3,720 if Bob starts at 70, all the way down to $2,250 if Bob starts at 62. Yes, yes, I know this subject matter is about as much fun as the heartbreak of psoriasis.

Employment

If you plan to keep working after you start collecting your Social Security, you'll be happy to know that you may be in jeopardy of forfeiting some of your benefits. Here's the deal, you can only make so much income through your employment before our very benevolent federal government decides THEY have the right to YOUR Social Security money. Outrageous, I know, but not totally surprising. In 2020, **if you are under full retirement age for the entire year**, the government will deduct $1 from your benefit payments for every $2 you earn above the annual limit of $18,240.

To make up for it, in the year you turn your FRA, they will ONLY deduct $1 for every $3 you earn above $48,600.

Once you get to your FRA, there is no income limit and, therefore, no forfeiture … yet. After all, we are talking about the government here; this could have already changed by the time you read this best seller.

Survivor Benefits

When Paul and Esther came into my office after hearing my radio show, they thought they had done a fairly good job of planning their retirement income. Upon closer examination, however, they had overlooked one critical consideration: What happens to their Social Security income when one of them dies?

They were surprised to learn that when the first spouse heads to greener pastures, the surviving spouse will retain either their own benefit or that of their spouse, whichever is higher.

In Paul and Esther's case, where both of their benefits were about the same amount, that meant a 50% decrease in their Social Security income upon the first of their deaths. Fortunately, we were able to establish a private pension for them that would pick up the slack when the time came.

By the way, the amount of the survivor benefit is another thing to think about when determining whether you should delay taking your benefits. If Social Security will be a large part of your and your spouse's retirement income, and if there is a big difference between your and your spouse's benefits **and** if you can afford to wait, it may not be a bad idea. Waiting ensures that the surviving spouse will receive a larger payout.

One more important point on survivor benefits: A surviving spouse must be at least age 60 before they can collect on their deceased spouse's benefit. This very thing came up when I visited with the Martin's the other day. Mr. Martin was 73, and his trophy wife, Mrs. Martin, was a mere 41. If he should happen to die before Mrs. Martin reaches age 60, she would not be eligible for any of his Social Security benefits. I couldn't tell for sure, but upon hearing this, I detected that Mrs. Martin might have been rethinking the wisdom of the whole sugar daddy thing.

But guess what? Once again, yours truly rode in on his white horse and saved the day (and maybe their marriage) by doing some creative planning, enabling Mrs. Martin to receive $1,000,000 tax-free, when Mr. Martin checked into the Horizontal Hilton. It didn't occur to me until much later that I may have put Mr. Martin's life at stake by implementing this plan. Hopefully, Mrs. Martin does not have any homicidal tendencies or mob connections.

Anyway, if you find yourself on the younger side of a significant age disparity between you and your spouse, we may need to discuss some options that will allow you to at least maintain your standard of living when your spouse passes. The Social Security survivor benefit may not do the trick. Of course, you'll first have to convince me that you don't have any nefarious intentions. That's reasonable, right?

Taxation of Social Security Benefits

That's right; I did not stutter. Your Social Security benefits may be subject to federal income tax. And this is AFTER you already paid tax on the income these benefits are based upon. You're not really surprised, are you? If so, you just don't understand the concept of government overreach.

So, here's the deal, in 2020, single filers earning $25,000 to $34,000 must pay income tax on 50% of their benefits. At $34,001 and up, you will pay income tax on 85% of your benefits. For married couples filing jointly, those numbers are 50% on $32,000 to $44,000. Up to 85% of your benefits are taxed if you are unfortunate enough to be among the super wealthy and earn over $44,000.

As with everything the government comes up with, there are approximately 10 million exceptions to these guidelines. But, since I am NOT a tax professional, I am going to refer you to one — either yours or ours if you'd like to get into detail about your specific situation.

For many of my clients, Social Security benefits are an integral part of their income throughout retirement. So, if you are not already collecting, rest assured that we will spend a fair amount of time on this incredibly tedious subject when you come in for your consultation. Occasional dozing during these sessions is completely normal and, well, expected.

"I'm stuck between, 'I need to save money' and 'you only live once.'"

— Anonymous

"Anyone who neglects to care for family members in need repudiates the faith. That's worse than refusing to believe in the first place."

1 Timothy 5:8

Chapter 12

Sorry, I Forgot My Wallet

First, let's clear something up, I AM NOT AN ATTORNEY *(I don't even play one on TV)*, AND YOU SHOULD NOT CONSIDER THIS CHAPTER LEGAL ADVICE. However, I do have a very well-known estate planning attorney here at Cornerstone Capital, and he is standing by, ready to assist you with your estate planning needs and questions. I will leave it to our attorney to get into the specifics of your situation, but let's at least cover some of the basics.

We have a saying around here that my colleague and professional speaker Mickey O'Neill came up with, which very simply sums up the need for an estate plan, "If you own something and you love someone, you plan." So, exactly what is estate planning? It is the process of anticipating and arranging for the management and distribution of your assets when you become permanently out of print while minimizing gift, estate, and income tax.

Part of estate planning is the establishment of a trust. Trusts come in many different shapes and sizes, but our attorney typically uses something called a revocable living trust. It is so titled because it is, well, revocable and controlled by you during your lifetime.

The primary reason for the establishment of a trust is to avoid a process called probate when you go on to the eternal redemption center.

I have a friend who always seems to forget his wallet when we go to dinner. It's either he lost it, forgot it, or the dog ate it. Regardless of his lame excuses, I'm left with the check. Well, becoming living impaired without a trust can be the equivalent of my friend forgetting his wallet, as your heirs are now "left with the check" (aka probate).

Having your heirs go through probate because you forgot your wallet is not the best way to express your love for them. In short, probate is a legal proceeding whereby a judge makes decisions on the distribution of your assets rather than you or your loved ones. And the process is about as much fun as running a marathon with sand in your underpants.

My father-in-law passed away in 2014 with about $50,000 to his name. As you might imagine, dolling out advice to your in-laws (or any relative for that matter) is not always well received. As a result, he had no trust, just an outdated do-it-yourself will that served no purpose. Six years later, we are STILL dealing with trying to get this settled. Oh, and here's the kicker; his $50,000 has magically turned into $20,000 because of attorney fees. Please don't let your loved ones experience a similar nightmare.

The differences between probate and a revocable living trust:

Probate	Revocable Living Trust
• Public record proceeding	• Private
• Takes effect at death	• Takes effect during your life and remains in effect after death
• Can take as long to complete as the Indian Cultural Museum	• Can usually be done relatively quickly
• Court supervised	• Trustee supervised
• Easy to contest	• Difficult to contest

A decent revocable living trust should be:

An ongoing process, not just a one-time event

Your plan needs to be reviewed and updated as your circumstances change. I often meet with folks who tell me they have an estate plan or trust. When I ask them when it was last reviewed, they either don't remember or tell me it was just after the Cuban Missile Crisis.

Reasons to update your trust:

✓ Your financial situation has changed significantly
✓ You've received an inheritance
✓ You or one of your children has gotten married/divorced
✓ You've had grandchildren
✓ You'd like to change the trustee(s) or co-trustee(s)
✓ You haven't reviewed your plan in five years or more
✓ A person designated to receive assets from your estate dies
✓ You or a family member becomes seriously ill

- ✓ You want to make significant charitable gifts
- ✓ You want to change when or how a beneficiary receives estate proceeds

Drawn up by an estate planning attorney

Notice I specified "estate planning" attorney, not just any run-of-the-mill general practice type. Estate planning is a complex and ever-evolving process, one that cannot be effectively executed by your nephew who knows "a little something" about it because he minored in law at Western Suburban College of Nursing.

Many years ago, my dad (RIP!) needed heart valve replacement surgery. He lived in Cedar Rapids, Iowa, so naturally, we first consulted with the local heart surgeon. Dad needed a quadruple valve replacement, a procedure this doctor had performed very few of, maybe three or four in his career.

My siblings and I were not thrilled with the prospect of my dad going under the knife by a relative novice. So, we scheduled an appointment at the Mayo Clinic in Rochester, Minnesota, which was only about a four-hour drive. What we discovered was amazing! Rather than having performed three or four in his career like the doctor in Cedar Rapids, the heart surgeon at Mayo did one or two of these operations each DAY! Where do you think dad had his surgery?

Here's the thing, your legacy is far too important to be handed over to a novice. Most attorneys who call themselves estate planners might do somewhere between 10-25 estate plans each year. At Cornerstone Capital, we routinely do over 100 estate plans every year, meaning we are intimately familiar with estate planning law and the sometimes intricate, ever-evolving, and critically important process of planning for your legacy.

Properly Funded

This can be a huge problem. So often, people go to the time and expense of putting together a trust but never fund it. Funding the trust means putting your various assets, real estate, investment accounts, life insurance, and so on into the trust. It could be as simple as changing a beneficiary designation on a life insurance policy or a bit more involved, like retitling an investment account. If we do your estate plan, you can rest assured that it will be properly funded, unless you go rogue and don't follow our advice!

During my first meeting with Dave and Susan, I asked them if they had a trust in place. They proudly said that they did and proceeded to extol the virtues of their lawyer and financial planner. I didn't think much of it until our next meeting when I looked at their statements. They had a few different accounts that were set up as joint tenants with right of survivorship, otherwise known as JTWROS accounts. These types of accounts allow the assets to pass from one person (usually spouses) to another upon the death of the first person without going through probate. So far, so good, right? Not so fast! Then I asked them another question.

"What happens if you are both killed in a car accident? Or what if one of you becomes incapacitated, and then the other one of you dies? Are you going to avoid probate under those circumstances with a JTWROS account?"

Unfortunately, they had no real clue what I was talking about. It looked to me as though the "professionals" they were dealing with had about as much experience with funding trusts as I have with successful dieting.

Verify this with your attorney and/or financial planner — assuming they are not the same nincompoops that Dave and Susan used — but, typically, if the trust is properly funded, the brokerage accounts will be owned by the trust rather than being set up as JTWROS accounts. Why? So the proceeds pass to the beneficiaries per the terms of the trust EVEN in the event of the previously mentioned car accident or incapacitation.

The point of the pretty much nonsensical last few paragraphs is that you can have the best trust on the planet, drawn up by Johnnie Cochran himself, but it will do little to avoid probate if it is not properly funded.

Include an advance directive

An advance directive is a legal document in which a person specifies what actions should be taken for their health if they are no longer able to make decisions for themselves due to illness or incapacity. If you find yourself in such a situation, do you want to be on life support? Do you want food, food and water, just water, or nothing at all? Do you wish to donate your organs? All of them or only those that you specify? With an advance directive, you make all of these decisions in advance, duh, so your loved ones don't have to leave it up to your doctors, or, worse yet, a judge to make these decisions if you are not able.

You may recall the case some years back of a young lady named Terri Schiavo. In 1990, at the age of 26, an otherwise healthy Schiavo suffered a heart attack after a fall down the stairs. She suffered massive brain damage and was declared to be in a persistent vegetative state.

After two years of unsuccessful attempts at physical, occupational, and speech therapy, Schiavo's husband Michael petitioned a Florida court to have her feeding tube removed, only to be vehemently opposed by Schiavo's parents. The parents argued that even under such dire, seemingly hopeless circumstances, Terri would indeed wish to live. After a 12-year court battle, Michael Schiavo finally prevailed, and Terri's feeding tube was removed.

She died a few days later, on March 31, 2005, 15 years after the nightmare began.

The sad part is that the entire ordeal could have been avoided if Terri had an advance directive in place that would have had explicit instructions on her wishes in such a situation. No lawsuits, no judges, no lawyers, no hundreds of thousands of dollars in legal fees, and, most importantly, no 15 years of misery and suffering for Terri and her loved ones.

Keep in mind, Terri was 26 years old when this tragedy occurred. How much more imperative and urgent is it to have an advance directive in place for old codgers like you and me?

Let me wrap up this incredibly stimulating chapter by saying this: If you own something and you love someone, you plan!

"I like to think money won't change me; yet when I am winning at Monopoly, I am a terrible, terrible person."

— Anonymous

"A sterling reputation is better than striking it rich; a gracious spirit is better than money in the bank."

Proverbs 22:1

Chapter 13

Let's Not Jump to Conclusions

Well, we've come a long way, haven't we? From the incompetence of a certain paperboy to the disposition of your assets when you become immortality challenged.

No doubt that you've conjured up many questions while reading this treasure (assuming you were able to keep your eyes open), and I would love to answer them for you in person.

Dianna and Steve came in to visit me several years ago after hearing my radio show. We discussed retirement planning basics and the importance of getting a plan in place now, as they were closing in on retirement. As sometimes happens, they did not see the urgency in taking action and put off making any kind of decisions, saying they'd get back in touch with me.

I never heard any more from them until a few months ago when Dianna called. After the normal pleasantries of the phone call, Dianna told me that Steve had been killed in a motorcycle accident while they were on vacation. After offering my condolences, I asked her if they had ever done anything in regard to putting a retirement plan together.

She said that just before they left on their motorcycle trip, she had been putting some pressure on Steve to get something in place. His response? "We'll take care of it when we get back." Unfortunately, Steve never came back.

As a result, Dianna was left holding the bag with a lot of loose ends, questions, concerns, and anxiety about her finances and supporting herself going forward, which was the purpose of her call, to see if I could offer my advice and counsel.

This tragic but all-too-common occurrence reminded me of the quote from Pablo Picasso, "Only put off until tomorrow what you are willing to die having left undone." It is human nature to put off important or uncomfortable decisions as we don't always recognize the consequences that can come with procrastination. Sometimes, as in this case, that indecision can lead to very undesirable effects for the loved ones we leave behind.

My friend Michael DeLon recently wrote an interesting piece entitled "Later Means Never," which I believe is an astute observation. How often do we say to ourselves or others, "I'll do it later," which most of the time translates to "I'll do it never"?

If you got past third grade, you have no doubt figured out that the purpose of telling you the cautionary tale about Dianna and Steve is to encourage you to act NOW. Whether your retirement plan is nonexistent, needs tweaking, or requires a complete overhaul, or if you simply want a second opinion, pick up your flip phone or get on your dial-up internet and contact us to schedule a meeting. Some of you reading this drivel have already had your initial consultation with me. In that case, I encourage you to keep moving forward until all the t's are dotted and the i's are crossed. See what I did there?

Thank you for your indulgence of my very deficient writing ability. I look forward to seeing you soon!

About the Author

Who's this guy with the smirky smile?

Yep. You guessed it.

That's me.

Instead of having you read a boring bio, I thought you'd enjoy watching a short video to get to know me better:

Scan the QR code using your smartphone's camera to open the website.

Or just type this into your browser:

https://www.okcornerstone.com/get-to-know-me.html

Thanks for reading my book. I look forward to serving you.

Derek

Even More About the Author

As longtime host of the "Safe Money Radio" show and president and founder of Cornerstone Capital Management, Derek Colton has enjoyed helping clients from all walks of life protect and grow their hard-earned retirement money.

Derek likes to "brag" that as a layman, he made every investing mistake known to man — some of them many times. These costly mistakes inspired Derek to educate himself on the intricacies of the financial markets and the pros and cons of various financial products and investment strategies.

He founded Cornerstone Capital Management, a retirement and investment planning firm, to do what he could to help others avoid the investing blunders he made early on. He uses his experience to assist his clients in planning, sustaining, and enjoying a secure retirement.

Derek specializes in working with those who are either retired or close to retirement, utilizing strategies specifically designed to help mitigate or even eliminate downside stock market risk while continuing to capitalize on market uptrends. He likes to say that the purpose of employing these strategies is to help his clients SWAN (Sleep Well at Night).

Derek lives a full life near Edmond, Oklahoma, surrounded by:

- Five daughters (and grandkids)
- Four sons-in-law
- Three shirts that actually fit (the shirt in the photo isn't one of them)
- Two dogs
- One amazing and very tolerant wife of 37 years, and
- Zero extra bedrooms

Derek Colton
Cornerstone Capital Management
2569 S. Kelly
Suite 100
Edmond, OK 73013

(405) 444-9067

Derek@okcornerstone.com

www.okcornerstone.com

Made in the USA
Monee, IL
05 August 2023

40466805R00075